THE ESSENTIAL
MADHUR JAFFREY

THE ESSENTIAL MADHUR JAFFREY

EBURY PRESS
London

Madhur Jaffrey is perhaps the most popular figure in Indian cookery today. She was born in Delhi, India and began her career as an actress. She published her first cookery book, *An Invitation to Indian Cooking*, in 1974 and since then has written several others, including *Madhur Jaffrey's Cookbook* and *Eastern Vegetarian Cooking*. However, it was her eight-part cookery series for BBC Television, entitled *Madhur Jaffrey's Indian Cookery*, first aired in 1982, which made her a household name. She is now widely acknowledged as the finest authority on Indian food and cookery. She lives in New York.

First published in 1996

1 3 5 7 9 10 8 6 4 2

Copyright © 1973 and 1981 Madhur Jaffrey
This new edition copyright © 1996 Madhur Jaffrey

First published in the United Kingdom in 1996 by Ebury Press
Random House, 20 Vauxhall Bridge Road, London SW1V 2SA

Random House Australia (Pty) Limited
20 Alfred Street, Milsons Point, Sydney,
New South Wales 2061, Australia

Random House New Zealand Limited
187 Poland Road, Glenfield, Auckland 10, New Zealand

Random House South Africa (Pty) Limited
PO Box 337, Bergvlei, South Africa

Random House UK Limited Reg. No. 954009

A CIP catalogue record for this book is available from the British Library.

ISBN 0 09 180677 1

Designed by The Senate and Bob Vickers

Printed and bound in Great Britain by Mackays of Chatham plc, Kent

The recipes which appear in this book were previously published in *Eastern Vegetarian Cooking* and *An Invitation to Indian Cooking*.

CONTENTS

INTRODUCTION

Although Indian restaurants have flourished in this country for many years, many of these establishments do not do justice to the richness of traditional Indian cookery. The greatness of India's cuisine lies in its regional foods and menus. Yet, sadly, many of the Indian restaurants in Britain underplay the uniqueness of a regional cuisine and end up by producing a generalised Indian food from no particular area, or falling back solely on popular dishes such as tandoori chicken or lamb korma.

This is, of course, not true of all Indian restaurants but I am still left with the impression that the only way to superb Indian food, with a guarantee of variety, quality and freshness of ingredients, is to learn to cook it for yourself. And that is the purpose of this book - to open up the infinite possibilities offered by a cuisine that is over a thousand years old. The increasing popularity of Indian food in this country has meant that specialist ingredients are now more widely available and the spices that are used again and again in Indian cookery are sold in most supermarkets. Many greengrocers and market stalls now sell fresh produce such as fenugreek greens, okra and ginger.

Many of the recipes in this book are ones which I learnt from my mother. I longed to learn to cook and when I was a student in England I wrote home demanding recipes for my favourite dishes. With a willingness to experiment I tried out the handed-down recipes, adapting them according the ingredients and cooking methods that were available in Britain. I learnt that instead of roasting aubergines in hot ashes as my mother had done, I could do it just as well over a gas burner, that a food processor could do more quickly and efficiently what an Indian grinding stone did. I managed to create traditional dishes with a true taste of India, but often had to take an unorthodox route to get there.

In this book I have gathered together some of my favourite recipes and hope that you will be inspired to experiment as I have done. Most of the recipes are quite detailed, discussing what each stage should look like, but don't be put off by long recipes. Some of the dishes are very quick and easy, some require more patience and time but all will, I hope, produce delicious and satisfying results.

SOUPS, SNACKS AND APPETIZERS

While India does not as a nation drink soup, we have, fortunately, many communities within the subcontinent that insist on being exceptions to the rule. The Anglo-Indians (a 300-year-old community with a mixed English and Indian heritage) make a delicious mulligatawny soup (a corruption of the Tamil words *milagutannir*, meaning 'pepper water') with meat and chickpea flour, and the Bohris of Gujarat make a superb 'white soup' (*safed sarvo*) with goat's meat and milk.

The appetizers you will find in this chapter are those among the Indian 'snack' foods that can be most conveniently eaten with drinks – triangular *samosas*, filled with meat or potatoes, vegetable fritters, and minced meat *kababs*. *Kababs*, often sprinkled with finely sliced onion rings, are favourites among Indian Scotch drinkers. The North Indian word for alcoholic beverages is *sharab*, and it is very interesting that the North Indian label for a man who drinks and eats well is *sharabi-kababi*!

Mulligatawny soup

Serves 4

Judging from the Tamil origin of the name 'mulligatawny' one might deduce that it originated in the Madras region 100 to 300 years ago under the benevolent gaze of British patronage. British in concept but Indian in its ingredients, this hearty soup became very popular with the Anglo-Indians scattered all across India, and there are probably as many recipes for it as there are Anglo-Indian families.

---

4 cloves garlic, peeled and chopped
a piece of fresh ginger, about 1 cm (1/2 inch) cube, peeled and chopped
225 g (8 oz) boneless lamb (from shoulder or leg), with fat removed, and cut into 2 cm (3/4 inch) cubes
2 tbsp vegetable oil
1 tbsp white poppy seeds, roasted and ground
1/2 tsp ground coriander
1/2 tsp ground cumin
1/4 tsp ground turmeric
1/2 tsp salt (more if the broth is unsalted)
1/8 tsp cayenne pepper (optional)
1/8 tsp freshly ground black pepper
2 tbsp chickpea flour (*besan*)
600 ml (1 pint) chicken broth (tinned or homemade)
1 tbsp lemon juice
2-3 tbsp cooked rice, or (1–1 1/2 tbsp) uncooked rice (optional)

Put the garlic and ginger into the container of an electric blender with 3 tbsp of water. Blend at high speed until you have a smooth paste. Set aside.

Pat dry the pieces of lamb. Heat the oil in a 2.3 litre (4 pint) pot over medium-high flame, and add the meat. Turn, and fry until the pieces are lightly browned on all sides. Remove with slotted spoon and set aside. Turn the heat off.

To the same pot, add the paste from the blender, the roasted and ground poppy seeds, the coriander, cumin and turmeric. Turn the heat to medium, and fry, stirring constantly, for about a minute. Turn heat to low.

Now add the browned meat and any juice that may have accumulated, the salt, cayenne and black pepper. Stir and leave on low flame.

Combine chickpea flour and 4 tbsp water in a bowl, mixing thoroughly until you have a smooth paste. Slowly add the chicken broth, stirring as you do so. Pour this mixture over the meat in the pot. Turn heat to high and bring soup to the boil. Add uncooked rice if you are using it. Cover, lower heat, and simmer gently for half an hour or until meat is tender. Stir in the lemon juice.

If you are using cooked rice, mix it into the soup just before serving. Pour the soup into a tureen or into individual bowls. Mulligatawny soup can be served with both Indian and Western-style meals. Since it is thick and fairly filling, it can be a main course for lunch or a light supper followed by a green salad and fruit.

Dal soup

Serves 8

My mother used to make this mild-flavoured 'split-pea' soup. The only spices in it were cloves, peppercorns, and turmeric. It was served with lemon wedges and homemade croûtons.

---

285 g (10 oz) green or yellow split peas, washed
1.4 litres (2¹/₂ pints) chicken broth (tinned or homemade)
24 black peppercorns and 15 whole cloves (tied in cheesecloth)
¹/₂ tsp ground turmeric
¹/₂–³/₄ tsp salt (more if broth is unsalted)

Garnish
8 lemon wedges
croûtons made from 6 slices of slightly stale bread and enough vegetable oil to cover 1–2 cm (¹/₂–³/₄ inch) in a 25 cm (10 inch) frying pan

---

Combine the split peas and chicken broth in a pot and bring to the boil. Remove scum from the top.

Add the spices in the cheesecloth, the turmeric and the salt. Cover, lower heat, and simmer gently for 1 to 1¹/₂ hours or until peas are tender. Remove cheesecloth from soup, squeeze its juices into soup, and discard. Check salt.

Press the soup through a strainer, using the back of a wooden spoon, or put it through a food mill. If the soup seems too thick, add a little water.

To serve: Heat soup. Serve in bowls, garnished with a lemon wedge. Pass around croûtons on the side.

To make croûtons: (These can be prepared ahead of time.)

Remove crusts and cut slices of bread into 1 cm (¹/₂ inch) cubes.

Heat oil in a frying-pan over medium flame, and put in a third of the croûtons. Fry for 3 or 4 minutes, turning them around, until they are golden brown. Lift out with slotted spoon and leave to drain on paper towels. Prepare the rest of the croûtons in two more batches, and leave to drain.

My cream of tomato soup

Serves 4–6

Cream of tomato soup has been adopted by India with a passion. The same small coffee houses that offer the most traditional *dosas* and vegetable *pakoris* also have, to the surprise of many tourists, tomato soup on their menus. When cooking tomato soup in their homes, most Indians cannot resist putting in a few spices or herbs. My sister-in-law, for example, puts in fresh curry leaves from the tree that grows just outside her kitchen door. The soup immediately becomes very aromatic. Here is my tomato soup, which can be had hot or cold.

675 g (1½ lb) ripe tomatoes, chopped
1 tbsp dried, sliced lemon grass
1 tbsp dried or fresh curry leaves
1 slice fresh ginger
1¼ tsp salt
4 tbsp unsalted butter
2 tbsp plain white flour
100 ml (4 fl oz) single cream

600 ml (1 pint) milk
½ tsp ground roasted cumin seeds
1/16–1/8 tsp freshly ground black pepper
1/8 tsp cayenne pepper
2 tsp lime or lemon juice
1 tbsp fresh finely chopped green coriander

Combine the tomatoes, lemon grass, curry leaves, ginger, ½ tsp salt and 100 ml (4 fl oz) water in a 2.8 litre (5 pint) pot and bring to the boil. Cover, lower heat, and simmer gently for 15 minutes. Uncover, turn heat to medium, and simmer a little more aggressively for another 15 minutes. Put the tomatoes through a sieve. You should have about 500 ml (16 fl oz) of thick tomato juice. Bring this juice to a simmer and keep on a very low flame.

Melt the butter in a heavy saucepan. Add the flour. Stir and cook the flour on low heat for 2 to 3 minutes. Do not let it brown. Now pour in the hot tomato juice, stirring all the time. Add the cream and the remaining ¾ tsp salt. Stir to mix and bring to a simmer. Add all the other ingredients except the fresh coriander. Stir to mix. Heat over a medium flame. As soon as the soup is about to come to the boil, turn off the heat. Ladle the soup into warmed soup bowls and serve garnished with a little chopped fresh coriander. If you wish to serve the soup cold, stir it occasionally as it cools so it does not form a thick film. Then cover and refrigerate.

Potato soup

Serves 4

---

1 tbsp vegetable oil	2 medium-sized potatoes, peeled
a pinch of ground asafetida or a	and quartered
1 mm (1/16 inch) pebble broken	2 tbsp tomato purée
from the chunk asafetida	1/4 tsp ground turmeric
1/4 tsp whole cumin seeds	11/4 tsp salt
	1/8 tsp cayenne pepper (optional)

Heat the oil in a 3.4 litre (6 pint) pot over a medium flame, put in the asafetida and the cumin, and stir once. In a few seconds, when the cumin seeds begin to sizzle, add the quartered potatoes, tomato purée, turmeric, salt and cayenne. Stir, and continue to fry for 2 minutes.

Add 1 litre (13/4 pints) of water and bring to the boil. Cover and simmer gently for 45 minutes.

Turn off heat and lift cover. Mash potatoes coarsely with a potato masher or with the back of a slotted spoon.

To serve: Pour soup into small bowls and serve.

Cold yogurt soup

Serves 4

Here is a very refreshing summer soup.

---

300 ml (1/2 pint) plain yogurt	4 tbsp peeled and grated cucumber
150 ml (1/4 pint) double cream	10–12 fresh mint leaves, finely
1/3–1/2 tsp salt	chopped
a sprinkling of freshly ground black	
pepper	

Combine all ingredients in bowl with 150 ml (1/4 pint) of cold water. Mix well. Cover and chill for several hours until ready to serve.

To serve: Serve on hot days in small chilled bowls.

Khatte aloo (sour potatoes)

Serves 10–12

This is an adaptation of a street-side snack to be found in different forms all over North India.

---

7 medium-sized potatoes, boiled
   ahead of time, and set aside for
   at least 2 hours to cool
1½ tsp salt (or to taste)
2–3 tbsp lemon juice (or to taste)

2 tsp ground roasted cumin
¼ tsp freshly ground pepper
¼–½ tsp cayenne pepper
2 tbsp finely chopped fresh green
   coriander

Peel the cooled potatoes and dice them into 1 cm (½ inch) cubes. Place in large bowl. Add remaining ingredients. Mix well. Check to see if salt and lemon juice are in correct proportion.

To serve: Place potatoes on platter and stick with toothpicks. Serve with drinks.

Vegetable pakoris

Serves 6–8

These *pakoris* are vegetable fritters – similar to Japanese tempura. They are generally eaten with tea, but there is no reason why they cannot be served with drinks. I have specified potatoes in this recipe, but you could use cauliflower florets, onion rings or Italian peppers, cut in half lengthwise, instead.

The batter
115 g (4 oz) chickpea flour (besan),
   sifted
¼ tsp salt
¼ tsp ground turmeric
¼ tsp ground cumin
¼ tsp baking soda
⅛ tsp freshly ground pepper
⅛ tsp cayenne pepper (optional)

The filling
3 medium-sized potatoes, peeled
   (or other vegetables – see above)
vegetable oil, enough for 6.5–7.5 cm
   (2½–3 inches) in wok, karhai, or
   other utensil for deep frying
salt and pepper for sprinkling on
   cooked pakoris

P ut the chickpea flour in a bowl. Gradually mix in about 200 ml (7 fl oz) water, until you have a thickish batter – thick enough to coat the vegetables. Add the other batter ingredients and mix well.

Cut the potatoes into rounds 1 mm (1/16 inch) thick, and put into a bowl of cold water.

Heat oil over a low flame until hot but not smoking. Take a few potato slices at a time, wipe them dry, and dip them in the batter. Now drop them into the oil. Fry slowly, 7 to 10 minutes on each side, until they are cooked through and have turned a golden-brown. Remove with slotted spoon and drain on paper towels. Sprinkle with salt and pepper. Do all *pakoris* this way, never putting in more at one time than your deep-frying utensil will hold in one layer.

To serve: Serve pakoris while they are crisp and hot with either the Fresh Green Chutney with Coriander Leaves and Yogurt or Fresh Mint Chutney with Fruit. The chutney is used as a dip. If you're feeling lazy, tomato ketchup or Chinese duck sauce or a combination of soy sauce, white vinegar, grated fresh ginger, and a dash of Tabasco can be used as alternative dips.

Seekh kabab, flat style

Serves 8–10

This version of the ground meat *kabab* is excellent to serve with drinks and to take out on picnics. The meat and spices can be combined a night in advance and left, covered, in the refrigerator.

1/2 medium-sized onion, peeled and chopped

4 cloves garlic, peeled and chopped

3 tbsp lemon juice

4 tbsp chickpea flour (besan)

1.25 kg (21/2 lb) minced lamb or beef, minced three times

a piece of fresh ginger, about 2.5 cm (1 inch) cube, peeled and chopped

20 whole black peppercorns

10 whole cloves

seeds from 8 cardamom pods

1 fresh hot green chilli, sliced (optional)

1/2 tsp ground nutmeg

1/2 tsp ground cinnamon

1 teacup (loosely packed) chopped fresh green coriander

1 tsp ground cumin

1 tsp ground coriander

11/2 tsp salt

1/2 tsp cayenne pepper (optional – use as desired)

1 egg, beaten

5 tbsp melted butter

In the container of an electric blender, combine the chopped onions, garlic, ginger, peppercorns, cloves, cardamom seeds, green chilli, nutmeg, cinnamon and lemon juice. Blend at high speed until you have a smooth paste.

Heat a small iron frying-pan over medium flame. Put in the chickpea flour and stir until it is 2 or 3 shades darker. Remove from heat.

In a large bowl, combine the meat, the chopped green coriander, the contents of the blender container, the cumin, coriander, salt, cayenne and roasted chickpea flour. Mix well with your hands. Cover and refrigerate until ready to grill (overnight if convenient).

Take meat out of refrigerator 45 minutes before serving. Preheat grill.

Add beaten egg to meat and mix well.

Line a 25 x 38 cm (10 x 15 inch) baking tray with aluminium foil, and brush it with half the melted butter.

Spread the meat mixture in the tray: it should be 1 cm (½ inch) thick. Brush the top with the rest of the melted butter. Place under grill, 7.5–10 cm (3–4 inches) away from heat. Grill until golden brown, about 15 to 20 minutes. Remove with a bulb baster any liquid that may accumulate.

Cut meat into 4–5 cm (1½–2 inch) squares.

Serve hot, or cold, with Fresh Green Chutney with Coriander Leaves and Yogurt or Fresh Mint Chutney with Fruit.

Cocktail koftas

Serves 15

Follow recipe on page 45. Make the koftas smaller, about 2 cm (½ inch) in diameter. They can be made a day in advance, and then reheated.

When serving, keep koftas warm in chafing dish. Place toothpicks nearby to aid self-service.

Whole-wheat samosas

Serves 8–10

Samosas are deep-fried patties, filled with potatoes or ground meat. I have a simple version of them. This is how they are made. (For stuffing use recipe for Kheema, page 43.)

---

225 g (8 oz) whole-wheat flour
3 tbsp vegetable oil (plus a little
   extra for brushing on dough)

½ tsp salt
vegetable oil for deep frying, enough
   for 7.5–9 cm (3–3½ inches) in pot

Combine oil and flour and rub together. Add salt and mix. Add about 250 ml (8 fl oz) water, a little at a time, until you have a firm dough. Knead the dough well for 7 to 10 minutes, until smooth. Form into a ball. Brush with a little oil, and cover with a damp cloth. Set aside until ready for use.

Cook Kheema until it is very dry, with no liquid left at all. If any fat has accumulated, it should be discarded.

Divide dough into 28 equal balls. (Each ball makes 2 samosas, so you'll end up with about 60.) Flatten each ball and roll it out on a floured surface until it is 9–10 cm (3½–4 inches) in diameter. Cut each round in half. Taking one semicircle at a time, moisten half the length of the cut edge with a finger dipped in water. Form a wide cone with the semicircle, using the moist section to overlap (¼ inch) and hold it closed. Fill samosa three-quarters full with the stuffing. Moisten the inside edges of the opening and press it shut. Seal this end by pressing down on the outside with the tip of a fork, as you would a pie crust. Prepare the samosas this way and keep them covered with a plastic wrap.

When you are ready to fry them, heat the oil in a wok, karhai or a utensil for deep frying. Keep the heat at medium. When oil is hot, drop a samosa in to check the temperature. It should start sizzling immediately. Fry 2 to 3 minutes, or until it looks a warm brown. Remove with slotted spoon and drain on paper towels. Do all samosas this way. If they brown too fast, lower your heat.

They can be reheated in a 150°C (300°F) mark 3 oven.

To serve: Place samosas on platter and serve hot or warm with either Fresh Green Chutney with Coriander Leaves and Yogurt or Fresh Mint Chutney with Fruit. The chutney is used as a dip.

Pacific king prawns on toothpicks

Serves 4

5 cloves garlic, peeled and chopped	3 tbsp vegetable oil
a piece of fresh ginger, about 2.5 cm (1 inch) cube, peeled and chopped	3 tbsp tomato purée
	½ tsp ground turmeric
	1 tbsp lemon juice
675 g (1½ lb) Pacific king prawns peeled and deveined	¾ tsp salt
	⅛–¼ tsp cayenne pepper

Put the garlic and ginger in the container of an electric blender along with 3 tbsp water. Blend at high speed until you have a smooth paste.

Wash prawns well and pat them dry. Cut each prawn into 3 sections. Set aside.

Heat oil in 25–30 cm (10–12 inch) frying-pan over medium flame. When hot, pour in the paste from blender and fry, stirring constantly, for 2 minutes. Add tomato purée and turmeric. Fry and stir another 2 minutes. Add 4 tbsp water, the lemon juice, salt and cayenne pepper. Cover, and simmer gently for 2 to 3 minutes. (This much can be done in advance.)

Five minutes before serving time, lift off cover, put in the prawns, and turn heat to high. Stir and fry the prawns for about 5 minutes or until they just turn opaque.

To serve: Place on platter and stick toothpicks into each prawn piece. Serve hot.

Pappadums, or papars

Serves 8–10

Pappadums or papars can be bought in delicatessens in two basic varieties – spiced and unspiced. The spiced ones often have a liberal sprinkling of crushed black pepper in them. They are deep-fried in hot oil and served at cocktail parties. The frying takes just a few seconds. Papars cannot be fried too far in advance, as any moisture in the air tends to make them go limp and they should be crisp. Papars come in several sizes. The large ones can be broken in half and then fried. They expand a bit as they are cooked. Before you set out to make them, put a large platter, well lined with paper towels, beside the stove to drain the papars.

---

10 papars or pappadums	oil for deep-frying, enough for 5 cm (2 inches) in 25 cm (10 inch) frying-pan

---

Heat oil in frying-pan over medium flame. When hot, put in one papar. It should sizzle and expand immediately. (If it doesn't, your oil is not hot enough!) Turn it over, leave for a few seconds, and remove with slotted spoon. Place on platter with paper towels and drain. Do all papars this way, one at a time. If they begin to brown, your oil is too hot. Turn down the heat. The papars should retain their yellow colour.

To serve: Serve warm or at room temperature with drinks.

Fried, munchable mung dal

Makes 340 g /12 oz

As a child, this was one of my favourite snack foods. I would buy it in a little paper cone from the bazaar, empty it into my pockets, and then munch it quietly as I accompanied my mother on her shopping sprees. This is not a spicy snack. It is generally seasoned with just salt and, if one likes, some black pepper. Cayenne may be sprinkled over it, if one so wishes. And there is no particular time of the day when it is meant to be taken. Like peanuts, fried mung dal is eaten whenever one feels like eating it, as a snack or with drinks.

---

185 g (6½ oz) mung dal	**½ tsp salt**
vegetable oil for deep frying	**freshly ground black pepper to taste**

Pick over the dal and wash it in several changes of water. Drain. Soak the dal in 1.1 litres (2 pints) of water for 5 to 8 hours. Drain thoroughly. Dry off dal by rubbing gently in a towel.

Heat oil for deep frying in a wok over a medium flame. You should have a good 6.5 cm (2½ inches) of oil in the centre of the wok. Line two plates with kitchen paper and keep them beside you. Have a fine, medium-sized sieve handy that you can lower into the oil.

When the oil has heated, lower the sieve into it. Put two modest handfuls of dal into the oil in the sieve. The dal will begin to sizzle and the oil will bubble. When the sizzling and bubbling subside (about 1½ minutes), the dal should be a golden colour (not brown), crunchy, and done. Lift up the sieve, shake it gently to drain off the oil, and then empty the dal on to one of the two plates. Keep doing this until all the dal is cooked, dividing it up between the two plates.

Change the kitchen paper on the plates again and again until it no longer appears oily. You may also rub the top of the dal with kitchen paper. (But do this fairly quickly, as you should salt the dal while it is still hot.) Consolidate the dal on one plate, lined with fresh kitchen paper. Sprinkle with salt and pepper. Mix and allow to cool completely.

Put the dal in a jar and cover with a tight lid. If kept in a tightly lidded jar, the dal will stay fresh for several weeks.

Khari poori (savoury biscuits with peppercorns)

Makes about 50

These savoury, deep-fried 'biscuits' are made with a combination of whole-wheat and white flour. In Gujarat, khari pooris or 'salty pooris' are often studded with crushed black peppercorns.

These pooris are generally eaten as a snack, accompanied by lassi, buttermilk, or tea. They can be eaten plain, or they may be smeared with hot pickles or sweet chutneys (like the Apricot Chutney). Khari pooris have been a standard 'journey food' in India for centuries. You could take them on picnics or hiking trips. You could also serve them with drinks.

---

100 g (3½ oz) wheatmeal flour
15 g (4 oz) plain white flour
1 tsp salt
1 tbsp coarsely crushed black pepper

3½ tbsp vegetable oil or softened unsalted butter plus oil for deep-frying

---

Sift the wheatmeal flour, white flour and salt into a bowl. Add the black pepper as well as the 3½ tbsp oil or butter. Rub the oil or butter into the flour with your fingers until the flour resembles coarse oatmeal. Now slowly add very hot water – about 100 ml (4 fl oz) plus 3 tbsp – and begin to gather the flour together. Squeeze the dough into a ball. It should just about hold. Do not knead.

Break the dough into about 50 balls. Keep them covered with cling film or a lightly dampened towel.

Heat about 4-5 cm (1½–2 inches) of oil in any utensil for deep frying (an Indian karhai or Chinese wok is an ideal utensil for this) over a medium flame. While the oil is heating, begin to roll out the pooris. Take each dough ball, flatten it, and roll it into a very rough round, about 5 cm (2 inches) in diameter. (Don't worry about the cracked edges.) Roll and fry as many pooris as your frying utensil will hold in a single layer. Fry 2 to 3 minutes on each side or until pooris are lightly browned on both sides and crisp. Adjust heat, if necessary.

Remove pooris with a slotted spoon and drain on kitchen paper. Make all pooris this way. Allow them to cool and then store them in an airtight container. Khari pooris do not need refrigeration and will stay fresh for several weeks.

FISH AND SHELLFISH

With improved refrigeration some seafood is now available in all the major cities of India. While availability of molluscs remains limited to the coast, prawns of varying sizes, lobster, pomfret, *rahu* and *singhara* can be found even in Delhi. And pomfret is, in my family, easily the most popular fish. It is a flat salt-water fish, on an average about 20 to 23 cm (8 to 9 inches) long, with its skeletal structure so obligingly designed as to make filleting a pleasure and eating a bone-free ecstasy. Its flesh is tender but firm, flaking delicately when cooked. The pomfret can be fried, baked, grilled, or cooked in banana leaves or green chutney. It is served at lunches, dinners, and official banquets.

Unfortunately, neither the pomfret nor the *rahu* and *singhara* mentioned earlier are available in Britain. What I will do in this chapter is to give you Indian recipes adapted for fish normally found in British fish markets. The recipes for prawns and lobsters remain basically unchanged, but I have modified some of the pomfret recipes and used them for the sea bass, mackerel, and the flounder. Instead of *rahu*, I have used cod. You could also use carp.

Coconut palms fringe most of India's coast from Bombay down to Cape Comorin and up again to Calcutta. Quite naturally, therefore, the fish caught along there are often cooked with grated coconut or with the 'milk' obtained from soaking freshly grated coconut in water. In Bengal, where the populace has rioted when fish was temporarily unavailable, a paste made out of ground black mustard seeds is often added to fish to give it a very special nose-tingling pungency. Moghul recipes from North India call for neither mustard seeds nor coconuts, but often for northern spices like saffron.

I need hardly stress that fish must be bought fresh – the eyes must look bright and the gills very red. It must also smell fresh. Cook it until just done. Overcooking will make it disintegrate or – in the case of prawns and lobster – become hard and leathery.

How to peel and devein prawns

This is really not as tiresome as it sounds. The secret is to make yourself entirely comfortable as you go about the task. Spread a double layer of newspaper at a table. Bring a clean plate, a sharp pointed knife, and a bag of prawns to the table.

Cut off the head of each prawn. Then pull off the legs that dangle on the belly side. Next, peel the shell from the body. It will come off in wide rings. Pull off the tail separately. To devein, make a shallow incision along the length of the prawn, right where the backbone would be if the prawn had one – all the way from head to tail. Here you will see a threadlike tube, often filled with black or green or yellow substance. Pull this out. If you don't find it, do not discard the prawn. It is still quite edible. Place all peeled and deveined prawns on a clean plate. Next, wash prawns thoroughly in cold running water and pat dry.

Marinated prawns with whole spices

Serves 6–8

Prawns are marinated in a paste of garlic, ginger, hot green chillies (or use cayenne pepper as a substitute), lemon juice, salt and pepper. They are then fried with a bay leaf, cinnamon, cardamom, cloves and peppercorns.

1.4 kg (3 lb) prawns (large prawns are particularly good for this recipe)

10 cloves of garlic, peeled and coarsely chopped

a piece of fresh ginger, 5 cm (2 inches) long and 4 cm (1½ inches) wide, peeled and coarsely chopped

2 fresh hot green chillies, sliced (or use ¼–½ tsp cayenne pepper as substitute)

3 tbsp lemon juice
1 tsp salt
1/8 tsp freshly ground black pepper
6 tbsp olive oil (or vegetable oil)
1 cinnamon stick, 6.5–7.5 cm
   (2 1/2–3 inches) long
5 cardamom pods

6 whole cloves
10 whole peppercorns
1 bay leaf
1/4 tsp ground turmeric

Garnish
2 spring onions

Peel and devein prawns. Wash under cold running water. Drain and pat dry as thoroughly as you can.

In the container of an electric blender, combine the garlic, ginger, green chillies, lemon juice, salt and freshly ground pepper. Blend at high speed until you have a smooth paste.

In a bowl, combine the prawns and the paste from the blender. Mix well. Cover. Leave, unrefrigerated, for an hour. If you wish to leave it longer (2 to 4 hours is fine), put bowl in the refrigerator.

Ten minutes before serving, heat the oil in a 25–30 cm (10–12 inch) frying-pan over a high flame. Add the cinnamon, cardamom, cloves, peppercorns and bay leaf. Stir for 10 seconds or until bay leaf darkens. Then put in the prawns and marinade and let this mixture bubble and cook, stirring constantly, only until the prawns turn pink and opaque all over. Remove them (and any whole spices that cling to them) with a slotted spoon and place them in a bowl. Add turmeric to contents of frying-pan. Keep cooking the marinade mixture over high flame, stirring all the time, until it becomes thick and paste-like. This will take just a few minutes. Now put the prawns back into the frying-pan. Stir around until the prawns are well coated; there should be no sauce left in the frying-pan. Check the salt. You may need to sprinkle on a bit more. Turn off heat.

To serve: Place the prawns on a warm platter. Wash the spring onions and slice into fine rounds, including at least an inch of the green part as well, and sprinkle them over the prawns. Serve with a rice dish, some kind of lentils, a vegetable and a yogurt dish. Warn people not to bite into the whole spices.

Prawns with crushed mustard seeds

Serves 3–4

---

450 g (1 lb) prawns
1 tsp black mustard seeds, crushed
   (use heavy mortar and pestle,
   coffee-grinder or grinding stone)
1/8 tsp ground turmeric
2 tsp tomato purée
4 tsp mustard oil (or any other
   vegetable oil)
2 cloves of garlic, peeled

2 slices of fresh ginger, 2.5 cm
   (1 inch) long, 2.5 cm (1 inch)
   wide, and 1 mm (1/16 inch) thick,
   peeled
1 hot dried red pepper
3/4 tsp salt
1/8 tsp freshly ground pepper
1 tbsp lemon juice

Peel and devein the prawns. Wash under cold running water. Pat dry as thoroughly as you can.

In a cup, combine the crushed mustard seeds, turmeric, tomato purée and 3 tbsp of water. Set aside.

Heat the oil in a 25–30 cm (10–12 inch) frying-pan over a medium-high flame. When hot, put in the cloves of garlic, the ginger slices and the hot red pepper. Stir and turn around. In a few seconds, as soon as contents begin to darken, add the prawns. Keep stirring until the prawns turn pink and opaque. Now put in the mustard seed paste. Turn heat to a moderate low. Keep stirring. Add the salt, pepper and lemon juice. Stir and fry another 2 minutes. Turn off heat.

To serve: Place on heated platter and serve with a rice dish or with hot pooris. Serve one or two vegetables with it, perhaps cabbage and peas, as well as a yogurt relish.

Prawns with peas and green coriander

Serves 3–4

---

450 g (1 lb) prawns	4 tbsp olive oil (or vegetable oil)
1 tbsp lemon juice	1/4 tsp ground turmeric
salt	3 tbsp tomato purée
freshly ground pepper	5 tbsp minced fresh green
5 cloves garlic, peeled and coarsely	coriander
chopped	1 small (or 1/2 large) sweet green
a piece of fresh ginger, 2.5 cm	pepper, cut in 0.5 cm (1/4 inch)
(1 inch) long and 2.5 cm (1 inch)	squares
wide, peeled and coarsely	1/2 teacup freshly shelled peas
chopped	1/8-1/4 tsp cayenne pepper (optional)

Peel and devein the prawns. Wash under cold running water. Pat dry. Sprinkle lightly with salt and pepper.

Place the garlic and ginger in the container of an electric blender, along with 3 tbsp of water. Blend at high speed until you have a smooth paste.

Heat the oil in a 25–30 (10–12 inch) frying-pan over a medium-high flame. When hot, put in the prawns. Fry and stir the prawns until they barely turn pink and opaque all over. Remove them to a bowl with a slotted spoon.

Into the same frying-pan pour the paste from the blender. Add the turmeric and fry, stirring, over medium heat for about 2 minutes.

Lower the heat and add tomato purée, coriander, green pepper, peas, lemon juice, salt and pepper to taste, cayenne pepper and 3 tbsp of water. Bring to the boil, cover, and simmer gently for about 5 minutes or until peas are just cooked.

Remove the cover from the frying-pan, raise heat, and boil away most of the liquid. When a thick paste-like sauce remains, put the prawns back in. Stir and cook until the prawns are well coated (there should be almost no sauce left in the pan). Taste, and add more salt if necessary. Turn off heat.

To serve: Place in a warm dish and serve with hot pooris, chapatis, or parathas, or with any kind of rice dish. You could also have a sauced potato dish, e.g. Potatoes with Asafetida and Cumin or, if you like, Mushrooms with Cumin and Asafetida.

Prawns with dill and ginger

Serves 4–6

---

a piece of fresh ginger, about
   2.5 cm (1 inch) cube, peeled and
   coarsely chopped
4 tbsp vegetable oil
1/2 tsp whole black mustard seeds
1 fresh hot green chilli, finely sliced
   (use more or less as desired)
1 tsp ground coriander

1 tsp ground cumin
1 tsp garam masala
1 tsp salt
1 tsp lemon juice
2 teacups fresh dill, washed and
   trimmed
900 g (2 lb) medium-sized prawns,
   peeled and deveined

Place the ginger in the container of an electric blender along with 3 tbsp water. Blend until smooth.

Heat the oil in a 25–30 cm (10–12 inch) frying-pan over medium flame. When hot, put in mustard seeds. As soon as they begin to pop (10 to 15 seconds), add the following at intervals, continuing to stir and fry over medium heat: first, the paste from blender; after a minute, the green chilli, adding a teaspoon of water if the mixture sticks; then the coriander, cumin, *garam masala*, salt, lemon juice; and after another 2 minutes, the dill and 150 ml (1/4 pint) of water. Bring to the boil. Cover, lower heat, and simmer for 10 minutes.

Pat the prawns dry and add to frying-pan. Turn heat to high, stir well and cook until prawns turn opaque, about 5 minutes.

To serve: Serve with plain rice and a salad. A relish with tomato or onion in it would also go well with it.

Prawns, crab, or lobster, Kerala style

Serves 4–6

This dish comes from Kerala, a state along India's southwestern coast. Roasted coconut is added to the seafood to give it a thick, dark sauce. It is quite delicious.

3 tbsp vegetable oil

2 medium-sized onions, peeled and finely chopped

a piece of fresh ginger, about 0.5 cm (1/4 inch) cube, peeled

4 cloves garlic, peeled and chopped

1/2 teacup grated and roasted fresh coconut

1/2 tsp ground turmeric

1 tbsp ground coriander, roasted

1/4 tsp cayenne pepper

3 tbsp tamarind paste

3 medium-sized tomatoes (tinned or fresh), peeled and chopped

1/2–3/4 tsp salt

900 g (2 lb) medium-sized prawns, peeled and deveined, or 900 g (2 lb) uncooked lobstermeat, cut into 2.5 cm (1 inch) pieces, or 900 g (2 lb) uncooked crabmeat, cut into bite-sized sections

Heat oil either in deep 25 cm (10 inch) frying-pan or in 25 cm (10 inch) heavy-bottomed pot over a medium-high flame. Put in the chopped onions and fry, stirring, for 7 to 8 minutes or until the onions are slightly browned, but soft. Turn off heat.

In a blender container combine the ginger, garlic, tomatoes, and grated roasted coconut. Blend at high speed until you have a paste. Add contents of blender container to frying-pan or pot. Also add the turmeric, coriander, cayenne, tamarind paste, salt and 150 ml (1/4 pint) water. Bring to the boil. Cover, lower heat, and simmer gently for 5 minutes.

(This much of the recipe can be made up to a day in advance. Keep covered and refrigerated until ready for use.)

Seven to 8 minutes before serving, bring the sauce to the boil. Add the prawns or lobstermeat or crabmeat, fold in, and cook at high temperature, stirring continuously, until the meat turns opaque (about 5 minutes). The sauce should be very thick and cling to the meat, but if you desire a thinner sauce, add a bit more water.

To serve: Place in warm bowl and serve with a rice dish and some kind of dal.

Baked sea bass with yellow rice

Serves 4–6

Pomfret is normally used in this recipe but it also seems to work very well with sea bass. A paste of onion, ginger, garlic and turmeric is first browned in oil. The fish is covered with it and then baked. The yellow rice is served on the side.

---

1 sea bass, 1.6–1.8 kg (3½–4 lb), cleaned thoroughly, with head and tail still on

1 medium-sized onion, peeled and coarsely chopped

a piece of fresh ginger 5 cm (2 inches) long and 2.5 cm (1 inch) wide, peeled and coarsely chopped

6 cloves garlic, peeled and coarsely chopped

½ tsp ground turmeric

4 tbsp olive or vegetable oil

¼ tsp whole cumin seeds

150 ml (¼ pint) tomato sauce (see p 114)

3 tbsp chopped fresh green coriander; reserve a bit for garnishing (as substitute, use regular parsley or fresh dill)

¾ tsp salt

⅛ tsp freshly ground pepper

⅛–½ tsp cayenne pepper (optional)

¼ tsp ground cloves

2 tbsp lemon juice

Preheat oven to 200°C (400°F) mark 6.

Wash the fish thoroughly in cold running water and pat dry, inside and out.

Place the onion, ginger, garlic, turmeric, and 4 tbsp of water in the container of an electric blender. Blend at high speed until you have a smooth paste.

Heat oil in 20–25 cm (8–10 inch) frying-pan over medium flame, put in the whole cumin seeds, and as soon as they darken add the paste from the blender. Fry, stirring, for 5 or 6 minutes. Now add the tomato sauce and green coriander. Cook, stirring, another 2 to 3 minutes. Remove frying-pan from heat. Add salt, pepper, cayenne, cloves and lemon juice, stir, and leave to cool slightly. (Check the salt in the paste. Remember it has to be enough to season *all* of the fish.)

Cut 4 diagonal slits, at the same angle as the gills, on each side of the fish. Distribute paste inside fish, over fish, and inside the slits. Place fish on baking platter or on baking tray covered with aluminium foil, and bake for 40 to 50 minutes, basting every 8 to 10 minutes. Meanwhile, prepare the Yellow Rice.

1 tbsp vegetable oil	¹/₂ tsp ground turmeric
¹/₂ tsp whole cumin seeds	1 tsp salt
340 g (12 oz) long-grain rice	

Heat oil in a 2.3 litre (4 pint) heavy-bottomed pot over medium heat. When hot, add cumin seeds. Stir a few seconds or until cumin seeds begin to darken. Add rice and turmeric. Mix and stir, fry for a minute, lower heat a bit if necessary. Add 750 ml (1¹/₄ pints) water and salt. Bring to the boil, cover, turn heat down very low, and cook, without lifting lid, for 30 minutes.

To serve: It is much easier if your baking dish is also your serving platter. This way there is less danger of breaking the fish. If you do need to move it, however, be very, very careful during the transfer. You can arrange the rice around the fish if the platter is large enough. If not, serve the rice separately and garnish your fish with freshly chopped green coriander. Serve with a green salad and sweet tomato chutney.

Sea bass in green chutney

Serves 2

Here is my version of a very popular dish in which the sea bass is smothered in green chutney and then cooked in banana leaves. Having no banana leaves handy, I use the prosaic but serviceable kitchen-aid – aluminium foil. It seems to work.

1 sea bass, 675–900 g (1¹/₂–2 lb) (with head and tail on, but otherwise cleaned)	2 tbsp olive or vegetable oil
	¹/₂ tsp whole black mustard seeds
	2 whole hot dried red peppers (optional)
a piece of fresh ginger, 2.5 cm (1 inch) long and 2.5 cm (1 inch) wide, peeled and coarsely chopped	¹/₂ tsp ground turmeric
	1 teacup chopped fresh green coriander
5 cloves garlic, peeled and coarsely chopped	2 tbsp lemon juice
	¹/₂ tsp salt

Clean and wash fish thoroughly under cold running water. Pat dry, inside and out.

Preheat oven to 200°C (400°F) mark 6.

Place the ginger and garlic in the container of an electric blender, along with 3 tbsp of water. Blend at a high speed until you have a smooth paste.

Heat oil in 20–25 cm (8–10 inch) frying-pan over medium-high flame, and add the mustard seeds. Within a few seconds, they will begin to expand and pop. Add the red peppers, and stir them once. Pour in the paste from the blender, add the turmeric, and fry, stirring, for about 2 minutes.

Pour contents of frying-pan into the blender. Add the green coriander, lemon juice and salt. Blend at high speed until you again have a smooth paste, adding up to 2 tbsp of water if necessary.

Line a large baking dish with a sheet of aluminium foil, large enough to fold over the fish. Cover the fish with the green paste, inside and out. Fold the foil over so the fish is completely enclosed in it. Place in the oven and bake for 30 minutes.

To serve: Remove fish carefully, place on warm platter, and serve with plain basmati rice. A tomato or onion relish would also go well with it.

Codfish steaks in yogurt

Serves 2

---

2 codfish steaks, 2 cm (³/₄ inch)
   thick (about 450 g (1 lb) of fish)
¹/₄ tsp ground turmeric
³/₄ tsp salt
3 medium-sized onions
6-8 cloves garlic
150 ml (¹/₄ pint) plain yogurt
freshly ground black pepper

¹/₄ tsp cayenne pepper (optional)
¹/₈ tsp sugar
6-8 tbsp vegetable oil
6 whole cardamom pods
2 cinnamon sticks, 5–6.5 cm (2–2¹/₂
   inches) long

Wash the codfish steaks. See that no scales adhere to skin. Pat them as dry as possible. Sprinkle steaks on both sides with the turmeric and 1/4 tsp of the salt, rubbing the seasonings gently in.

Peel the 3 onions. Chop 2 of them very finely and set aside. Chop the third one coarsely and place in the container of an electric blender.

Peel and chop the cloves of garlic. Put them in the blender container along with the yogurt, remaining 1/2 tsp salt, black pepper, cayenne and sugar. Blend at high speed until you have a smooth, thin paste.

Heat 5 tbsp of the oil in a 30 cm (12 inch) frying-pan over a medium flame. Put in the 2 steaks and sauté them lightly, about 3 minutes on each side, turning them over gently and carefully. (They should not get brown or crisp.) Remove with a spatula to a plate. Pour the oil from the frying-pan into a small bowl, leaving behind any sediment or pieces of fish.

Wash and dry the frying-pan. Measure the oil in the bowl and put it back in the clean frying-pan. Add more oil to make up 5 tbsp. Turn heat to medium, and when the oil is hot, put in the 2 finely chopped onions, the cardamom and the cinnamon. Fry the onions lightly, stirring, until they turn a light, golden-brown, about 5 minutes. Turn the heat down to low and pour in liquid from blender. Simmer (do not boil) on low heat for 10 minutes, stirring now and then.

Remove half of the sauce to a small bowl. Spread out the sauce in the frying-pan evenly, place codfish steaks on top, then pour the reserved sauce over them, spreading it evenly on top of the steaks. Cover and keep simmering at low temperature for about 10 minutes or until fish is cooked through.

To serve: I like to serve these steaks with plain boiled rice and a green salad with an oil and vinegar dressing, but you could choose any other rice dish and green beans, cauliflower, peas or okra.

Prawn pullao

Serves 6

This pullao can be cooked with prawns or with any firm-fleshed fish like cod or halibut (see following recipe).

---

340 g (³/₄ lb) fresh prawns	1 tbsp lemon juice
3 tbsp finely chopped fresh green coriander	¹/₂–1 fresh hot green chilli, finely sliced (optional)
1 tsp ground turmeric	4 tbsp vegetable oil
1 tsp garam masala	1 medium-sized onion
1¹/₂ tsp salt	340 g (12 oz) long-grain rice

Peel and devein prawns.

In a teacup, mix 1 tbsp warm water, the chopped green coriander, turmeric, garam masala, ¹/₂ tsp salt, the lemon juice and green chilli.

Heat 2 tbsp of oil in 25 cm (10 inch) frying-pan over medium-low heat. Pour in the contents of the cup and fry, stirring, for 2 to 3 minutes. Add the prawns, and on a medium flame fry them with the spices for about 4 minutes.

With a slotted spoon, remove the prawns to a covered dish, leaving the sauce behind. Pour 275 ml (9 fl oz) warm water into the frying-pan and scrape up all the spices stuck to the bottom and sides, turning up the heat if necessary.

Peel the onion, cut into fine rounds and cut rounds in half.

In a heavy-bottomed 3.4–4.5 litre (6–8 pint) pot, heat remaining 2 tbsp oil over medium heat. Put in the sliced onions, and fry them 3 to 4 minutes until the edges begin to turn brown. Now add the rice, 450 ml (³/₄ pint) water, 1 tsp salt and the liquid from the frying-pan. Stir and bring to the boil, then cover and reduce heat to very low. Cook for 25 minutes.

Lift the cover off the saucepan and add the prawns. Mix quickly with a fork and cover again. Cook another 5 minutes.

To serve: Serve with Cabbage with Onions and any yogurt side dish – Yogurt with Courgettes would be especially good.

Halibut or cod pullao

Serves 6

Follow the preceding recipe, only substitute halibut or cod for the prawns. Buy 340 g (12 oz) cod or halibut steaks or fillets. Make sure they are at least 1–2 cm (1/2–3/4 inch) thick. Cut the steaks or fillets into strips, each at least 4–5 cm (1 1/2–2 inches) long and about 2.5 cm (1 inch) wide.

To serve: Lift rice and fish gently out of pan and place on warm platter. You could serve it with Moong Dal, yogurt, and Chicken with Tomato Sauce and Butter.

Barbecued salmon steaks

Serves 6

---

6 salmon steaks, 2–2.5 cm
    (3/4–1 inch) thick
100 ml (4 fl oz) olive oil (or
    vegetable oil)
75 ml (3 fl oz) lemon juice
1 medium-sized onion, peeled and
    coarsely chopped
1 whole head of garlic, peeled and
    coarsely chopped
a piece of fresh ginger, about
    2.5 cm (1 inch) square, peeled
    and coarsely chopped

1–3 fresh hot green chillies (if
    desired), sliced, or 1/4–1 tsp
    cayenne pepper (if desired)
salt
1 tsp ground turmeric
freshly ground pepper

Garnish
2 lemons cut into wedges
6 sprigs fresh green coriander

In the container of an electric blender, place 2 tbsp of the olive oil, the lemon juice, and the chopped onion, garlic, ginger, green chillies or cayenne, 1 1/2 tsp salt, turmeric and 1/2 tsp pepper, and blend at high speed until you have a smooth paste (20 seconds).

(Note: If you are unsure of your ability to gauge how 'hot' it will turn out to be, first blend in half a green chilli, then the other half, then a whole, and so on. Taste a drop each time. Remember, though, that once the mixture is spread over the fish, it will taste only about half as hot.)

Place the marinade in a non-metallic bowl. Wash and pat dry the pieces of fish and place in marinade. Mix well, cover, and refrigerate for at least 2 hours. (Longer won't hurt.)

Heat the charcoal, keeping grill about 5–7.5 cm (2–3 inches) from fire. Next to stove place salt, pepper, the remaining olive oil and a pastry brush for basting.

When the fire is ready, brush the salmon steaks with oil and place on grill. Sprinkle the top with a little salt and pepper. Baste with oil. Let them grill until one side gets little brown patches (about 5 to 6 minutes). Turn over with a spatula and grill on the other side. Sprinkle top with salt and pepper. Baste again with oil. Cook another 6 minutes or until this side is also lightly browned. Remove.

To serve: Place on warmed platter and garnish with lemon wedges and green coriander.

MEAT

When an Indian sits down to eat meat, it is nearly always goat meat. It is usually *very* fresh goat meat and therefore not always very tender. Because of the lack of proper refrigeration facilities in India the animals are slaughtered daily and the meat is sold within 24 hours. In the richer homes it is then washed and refrigerated or frozen. But in the poorer homes it is cooked immediately. Since the meat is fairly tough, it is cooked slowly, over a longish period of time. For quicker fried and grilled dishes, the meat has to be tenderized first. The cheapest and most common tenderizer is crushed green papaya, but marinades of vinegar and yoghurt are also used.

Not only is Indian goat meat a little on the tough side; it is also very lean. The result is that we use a great deal of cooking fat to brown our meats. We tend to like this 'browned' look. When I buy lamb in Britain I first trim away all signs of fat. Then, to make it taste like the food I have in India, I cook it in lots of oil. This cooking fat can, of course, be removed later, once the dish is completely cooked, by spooning it off the top just before serving.

There is another significant difference in the quality of Indian meat which influences cooking techniques. In India, meat dropped into fat can be expected to fry, slowly or quickly, as the cook desires. Here, in Britain, if a pound of meat is put into oil to fry, unless one has taken careful preliminary steps, it will start boiling. The meat here gives off a lot of water, possibly because of prior freezing or because of the water-injecting habits of some butchers. There is no really good way to avoid this extra water, but defrosting frozen meat completely and wiping it well before cooking will be somewhat helpful. You can also fry the meat over a high flame in small quantities or boil off the extra liquid towards the end of the cooking time. As I go along I will tell you, in each recipe, which step to follow. What I want you to understand here is *why* an Indian meat dish cooked in Britain will never taste quite the same as it does in India.

Contrary to what most outsiders think, beef is eaten in India. About 80 per cent of India is Hindu (those who, technically, do not eat beef) but the other 20 per cent includes 60 million Muslims and 12 million Christians, i.e. 72 million people who can eat beef without battling with their consciences first.

When beef is cooked in the Indian manner, it is cooked slowly, over a period of time. In some areas, beef is dried and then fried with onions and served at breakfast. I have also eaten it cooked with spinach and with potatoes. One strange thing that I have noticed about us Indians is that although many Hindus will eat beef in restaurants, in Muslim and Christian homes, and when they are abroad, very few will cook it in their own kitchen. Each country has its own varieties of national hypocrisy. Self-righteously proclaimed rules on diet and cleanliness seem to be part of our heritage.

Beside beef, pork, lamb and venison are also eaten in the areas where they are found. *Dumba*, a fan-tailed sheep, is used for a special *pullao* (a rice and meat dish) cooked at the Muslim festival Id. Venison, considered rather dry, is often made into *koftas* (meatballs) or *shami kababs* (ground meat patties).

Meat is, of course, cooked very differently in the different regions of India. Most of my recipes are for dishes eaten in and around my home-town, Delhi. I will start with the easier recipes. My aim is to interest you first, and then entice you on – slowly.

Cuts of meat to use

Generally, when Indians cook a simple, everyday meat dish, they use meat with bone. This could come from the neck, shoulder, shank, ribs, or else-where from the goat or sheep. Often they combine these different parts, add some chunks from the leg, and throw in a few extra dark marrow bones for good measure. When I buy lamb in Britain for stew-type dishes,

I use all the cuts just mentioned. But I find that the English, eating with a knife and fork, do not seem to be much attracted to cubes of meat that are often three-quarters bone and one-quarter meat. When you eat with your hands, there is a great deal of pleasure to be derived from tearing meat off a bone with your teeth, and from sucking the bones. Since this is seldom done in Britain, I have limited myself a great deal to cubed, boned meat from shoulder of lamb. Any butcher will bone and trim the meat, but if you do not have access to a butcher you can buy shoulder chops from the supermarket and cut and trim them yourself. Just cut around the bones (these can be saved for soup), trim off the big concentrations of fat, and then cut the meat into 2.5–4 cm (1–1½ inch) cubes. Generally, you can assume a waste of about 40 to 50 per cent – so if you buy 1.8 kg (4 lb) of shoulder chops, you are likely to end up with about 900 g (2 lb) of meat or a bit more.

Leg of lamb can be used for a great many of the following recipes that require cubed meat, but it tends to get rather dry when cooked in a stew-like manner. It should be saved for grills and barbecues. However, if you wish to use it, cook it for the same length of time as meat from the shoulder – about an hour and fifteen minutes.

Neck and shank are excellent for stews but require longer cooking time – about 1½ to 2 hours. Serve them to people who like bones. You will need to buy about 1.8 kg (4 lb) to serve 4–6 since so much of it will be bone. You will also need to increase the salt a bit as some of it will be absorbed by the marrow.

Stewing beef may be substituted for cubed lamb. Here again, increase the cooking time, in this case to about 2½ hours, and adjust the recipes accordingly.

Khare masale ka gosht (meat with whole spices)

Serves 4-6

Here is my first meat recipe for this book. It is very easy to make and has a delicately flavoured taste. By placing it first, I hope to lure you all towards the more complicated and the more heavily spiced meat recipes. This dish is normally made with goat meat, using either the leg or the neck and shoulders, cubed into 2.5 cm (1 inch) pieces. You can, however, use either beef or lamb. If you use beef, get cubed stewing beef. If you use lamb, and don't want bones, get the butcher to give you 900 g (2 lb) of meat from the shoulder. Trim the larger chunks of fat from the meat, and cut it into 2.5 cm (1 inch) cubes.

---

8 tbsp vegetable oil
1 stick cinnamon, 5 cm (2 inches) long
20 whole black peppercorns
15 whole cloves
10 whole cardamom pods
2 bay leaves
1-4 whole dried hot peppers (or more, according to taste)

900 g (2 lb) boneless meat from shoulder of lamb, cut into 2.5 cm (1 inch) cubes, with fat and tissues removed
1–1½ tsp salt (according to taste)
1 tsp garam masala (optional)

Garnish
1 tbsp trimmed, chopped fresh green coriander

Pat the meat dry on paper towels.

Heat the oil in a heavy-bottomed pot over medium heat. When it is very hot, put the spices in quickly in this order: first the cinnamon, then black peppercorns, cloves, cardamom pods and bay leaves, and finally the hot peppers.

When the hot peppers begin to change colour and darken, add the pieces of meat and the salt. Stir for 5 minutes or until the pot begins to make boiling noises. Cover, lower heat, and cook for approximately 1 hour and 10 minutes – or until the meat is tender.

Remove the cover and continue cooking on medium heat for a final 3 to 5 minutes, gently stirring the meat pieces. Take care not to break them.

The meat is done now. It should look a nice brown, be tender, and have no sauce other than what is clinging to it and the fat it cooked in.

To serve: In India the contents of the pot are put into a serving bowl, 1 tsp of garam masala is sprinkled on the top, and the dish is served with hot chapatis or Rice with Spinach. I tend to think the English would be rather put off if they saw so much fat lining the serving dish, so I suggest that you lift the meat and spices out with a slotted spoon (the spices, though not to be eaten, make an attractive garnish). Place them on a serving platter and serve them sprinkled with chopped green coriander. You could serve almost any vegetable or dal as an accompaniment, or just plain rice. This dish can be made a day before, cooled, covered and refrigerated. Reheat gently and serve.

Pyazwala khare masale ka gosht (meat with whole spices and onions)

Serves 4–6

When I was a student in London and had written home begging my mother to teach me how to cook, one of the earliest letters I received from her was dated March 9th, 1956, with a recipe for the *Khare Masale Ka Gosht*.

Here it is, little changed from the recipe that my mother passed on to me. It's very much like the preceding recipe, with the addition of onions, ginger and cumin seeds, and it has one extra step.

900 g (2 lb) boneless meat from shoulder of lamb, with extra fat removed, cut into 2.5–4 cm (1–1½ inch) cubes	1 tsp whole cumin seeds
4 onions	1–4 whole hot dried red peppers (optional)
9 tbsp vegetable oil	5 whole black peppercorns
10 whole cardamom pods	1 piece fresh ginger, 4 cm (1½ inches) by 4 cm (1½ inches), peeled and minced or grated
4 whole large black cardamom pods (if available)	1 tsp salt (according to taste)
6–7 bay leaves	

Prepare all the ingredients first. Pat dry the meat pieces thoroughly with paper towel. Peel the onions, cut them in half, then slice in very thin half-circles.

Heat the oil in a 25–30 cm (10–12 inch) heavy-bottomed pot over medium heat. When it is very hot, put in the onions. Fry, stirring occasionally, for about 15 minutes or until the onions are a darkish brown and crisp, but not burned and black. Lift out the onions with slotted spoon, taking care that the fat drains back into the cooking pot first. Spread the onions on paper towels, and leave uncovered.

In the same pot, put in the small and large cardamoms, bay leaves, cumin, red peppers, peppercorns and finally the ginger. Stir for a minute until bay leaves turn dark and ginger sizzles awhile. Now add the wiped meat and the salt.

Stir for about 5 minutes or until the pot begins to make boiling noises. Cover, lower heat, and simmer very gently for 1 hour and 10 minutes or until meat is tender.

Take cover off, add onions, and let the meat cook over medium heat for a final 3 to 5 minutes, stirring gently. Take care not to break the meat. All extra liquid should be boiled away, and the meat should look a nice brown and have no sauce other than what is clinging to it, and the fat left in the pot.

To serve: See suggestions for preceding recipe.

Kheema (minced meat)

Serves 6

This is the first Indian dish all Indian students abroad learn to make. It can be cooked plain or with potatoes, peas or mushrooms.

---

2 medium-sized onions, peeled and coarsely chopped
4 cloves garlic, peeled and coarsely chopped
1 piece fresh ginger, 5 cm (2 inches) long and 2.5 cm (1 inch) wide, peeled and coarsely chopped
4 tbsp vegetable oil
1 stick cinnamon, about 5 cm (2 inches) long
4 whole cloves
4 black peppercorns

1 bay leaf
1–2 hot red peppers to taste (optional)
1 tbsp ground coriander
1 tsp ground cumin
½ tsp ground turmeric
1 large tinned tomato or 2 small ones, coarsely chopped
900 g (2 lb) finely minced lamb or minced beef
¾–1 tsp salt (or to taste)
1 tsp lemon juice

Place chopped onions, garlic and ginger in blender with 3 tbsp water and blend to smooth paste (1 minute). Set aside.

Heat oil in a 25–30 cm (10–12 inch) frying-pan over medium heat. When hot, add cinnamon stick, cloves, black peppercorns, bay leaf and then the red peppers. In about 10 seconds, when the peppers turn dark, add paste from blender, keeping your face averted. Fry for about 10 minutes, adding a sprinkling of water if the food sticks to the bottom. Add the coriander, cumin and turmeric, and fry another 5 minutes. Now put the chopped tomato in, fry for another 2 to 3 minutes, and add the minced meat and the salt. Fry on high heat for about 5 minutes. Break up all the lumps in the meat and brown it as much as you can. Add 150 ml (¼ pint) water and the lemon juice. Bring to the boil and cover. Lower flame and let it simmer for 1 hour.

To serve: Spoon off any accumulated fat and discard. Serve the kheema with rice, or chapatis, or parathas, and any vegetables you like.

Kheema with fried onions

Serves 6

This is easily my favourite kheema recipe. Nutmeg, mace and yogurt are added to the meat for a slight variation.

---

1 medium-sized onion, peeled and cut into very thin rings
4 tbsp vegetable oil
2 bay leaves
1 cinnamon stick, 7.5 cm (3 inches) long
6 whole cloves
2 medium-sized onions, finely chopped
a piece of fresh ginger, 2.5 cm (1 inch) long and 2.5 cm (1 inch) wide, finely chopped
5 cloves garlic, minced

1 tbsp ground coriander
1 tbsp ground cumin
1 tbsp ground turmeric
2 tbsp plain yogurt
1 medium-sized tomato (tinned or fresh), peeled and chopped
900 g (2 lb) minced lamb or minced beef
1/2 tsp ground mace
1/2 tsp ground nutmeg
1 tsp salt
1/4–1/2 tsp cayenne (optional)

Halve the onion rings and separate. Heat the oil in a heavy-bottomed 25–30 cm (10–12 inch) frying pan over medium heat. When hot, add the halved onion rings and fry them for about 5 minutes until they are dark brown but not burned. Remove with a slotted spoon and spread on paper towels. They will not be needed until the meat is almost cooked.

Put the bay leaves, cinnamon and cloves in the hot oil. When the bay leaves begin to darken and the cinnamon starts uncurling slightly, add the finely chopped onions, ginger and garlic. Fry, stirring, for 10–12 minutes, until the onions darken to a medium brown with darkish edges. Lower the flame a bit and add the coriander, cumin and turmeric. Fry for about 2 minutes, stirring all the time. Add the yogurt and cook, stirring, another minute. Now put in the chopped tomato, and keep frying and stirring for 2 to 3 minutes.

Add the meat. Raise the flame to medium (medium high if the meat is very watery) and fry, breaking up all the lumps with the back of a slotted spoon, for about 7 or 8 minutes. Next, put in the mace, nutmeg, salt, cayenne and 150 ml (¼ pint) water, and stir. Bring to the boil, cover, turn flame down to low, and let it simmer for 1 hour. Stir every 10 minutes or so. After an hour, mix in the browned onion half-rings and remove the cinnamon.

To serve: Serve with plain boiled rice, Moong dal and a cauliflower dish. This kheema is also excellent served with chapatis and pooris instead of rice.

Kheema with fried onions and peas

Serves 6

Follow the preceding recipe. Instead of cooking the minced meat for 1 hour, cook it for 50 minutes. Add 1 cup freshly shelled (or frozen) peas to it, mix, cover, and let cook another 5 to 10 minutes or until peas are tender. Add the fried onion half-rings and serve as in the previous recipe.

Koftas (Indian meatballs)

Serves 6–8 (makes about 48 meatballs)

Koftas take a fairly long time to make, so I suggest that you prepare them a day in advance. They can be covered and left in the refrigerator overnight (they will taste even better) and can be reheated before serving.

For the meatballs
900 g (2 lb) finely minced meat from a leg of lamb, or minced beef (put meat twice through fine blade of grinder, or ask your butcher to do so)
¾ tsp salt
¼ tsp freshly ground pepper
1 tbsp garam masala
1 tsp ground coriander
½ tsp ground cumin

For the stuffing
1–2 fresh hot green chillies (optional), finely chopped
2 cloves garlic, peeled and minced
a piece of fresh ginger, about 2.5 cm (1 inch) square, peeled and minced
6 spring onions, minced or 1 medium-sized onion, peeled and minced
3 tbsp lemon juice
a dash of salt and freshly ground pepper

For browning the meatballs
7 tbsp vegetable oil
**1 cinnamon stick, 5 cm (2 inches)
   long**
2 dried red peppers (optional)
4 whole cardamom pods
6 whole black peppercorns
4 whole cloves

2 tbsp ground coriander
2 tsp ground cumin
1 tsp ground turmeric
**2 medium-sized tomatoes (tinned or
   fresh), drained and chopped**
1 tbsp paprika
1 tbsp garam masala
1 tsp salt

For the sauce
**vegetable oil (as needed to make up
   5 tbsp)**
**4 medium-sized onions, peeled and
   coarsely chopped**
**6 cloves of garlic, peeled and
   coarsely chopped**
**a piece of ginger, 2.5 cm (1 inch)
   square, peeled and coarsely
   chopped**

Garnish
**1 tbsp chopped fresh green
   coriander**
1 onion, peeled and fried in rings
**1/4 tsp freshly ground cardamom
   seeds**

M ix all the ingredients for meatballs and keep covered in a bowl. Mix all the ingredients for the stuffing in another bowl.

Preparing the koftas takes a little time, so you might as well make yourself comfortable. If you have a table and chair in your kitchen, sit down there. Otherwise, spread a newspaper on any handy table and pull up a chair. Place before you the bowls of minced meat and stuffing, a platter with a cover, and a bowl of warm water.

The amount of meat specified in the ingredients will make about 48 koftas about 2.5–4 cm (1–1½ inches) in diameter. To simplify, portion the meat into 8 equal sections and then make 6 koftas out of each section.

Pick up enough meat for one kofta and form into a rough ball. Depress the ball and place a generous pinch of stuffing in its centre. Cover the stuffing by bringing around the meat from the outer edges and making it into a ball again. Smooth out the ball by moistening your palms and fingertips slightly and by working it in your hand. As each ball is made, place it on the platter and cover. Continue this way until you have used up all the meat and stuffing.

Heat the oil in a 25–30 cm (10–12 inch) frying-pan over medium heat, and put in the cinnamon, red peppers, cardamom pods, peppercorns and cloves. Stir once. In 10 seconds or so when the cloves begin to expand and the red peppers swell and turn dark, add the meatballs, just enough of them so they don't overcrowd the frying-pan. Brown them on all sides, remove with slotted spoon, and return to platter. (Remember, you are just browning the koftas, not cooking them through.) When all the koftas are browned, cover the platter and set aside.

The last step is making the sauce: Lift out the whole spices from the oil used for browning the koftas and place them with the koftas. Pour the oil into a very large and wide heavy-bottomed pot. Add more oil, if needed, to make 5 tbsp.

Place the chopped onions, garlic and ginger in a blender with 4 tbsp water and blend at high speed until you have a smooth paste.

Heat the oil, then pour in the paste from the blender. Fry over medium heat for about 15 minutes or until all the liquid has evaporated, stirring frequently. Add the coriander, cumin and turmeric, and keep frying for another 5 minutes. If the spices stick at the bottom of the pan, add 1 tsp of warm water at a time and keep stirring. (Never put too much water in. The idea is to fry the spices and onions, not to boil them.)

Add the chopped tomatoes, and continue to stir and fry 2 to 3 minutes. Add 1 tbsp water, cover pan, and let the tomatoes simmer 3 to 5 minutes, lifting the cover two or three times to make sure they are not burning. Remove cover, stir again, and fry for 1 more minute.

Now add 350 ml (12 fl oz) water, the koftas, the spices used in frying meatballs, the paprika, the garam masala, and the teaspoon of salt. Mix gently, and bring to the boil. Cover, and simmer slowly for half an hour.

To serve: Gently spoon out the koftas into a heated serving dish, taking care not to break them. Stir the sauce and pour it over them.

Sprinkle the green coriander and onion and cardamom on top. This dish can be served with plain boiled rice, Moong dal, and a cucumber and tomato salad, at its simplest.

At picnics, it goes well with 'stale' pooris or parathas and pickles.

Made a little smaller, the koftas can be served with drinks.

Warn diners not to eat the whole spices, but to leave them delicately on one side of their plate!

Nargisi koftas (large meatballs stuffed with hard-boiled eggs)

Serves 4

Koftas, as you know by now, are meatballs. *Nargis* is the Indian word for the narcissus flower. Why these particular meatballs are considered narcissus-like, I am not too sure. I can only guess that when cut in half (they are nearly always served that way) these egg-filled koftas remind some people of the yellow and white spring flower.

Nargisi koftas are definitely not an everyday dish in India but they are not difficult to make, look beautiful, and taste quite marvellous.

---

600 g (1¼ lb) minced lamb or minced beef (put through the mincer 3 times)
¼ tsp ground cloves
¼ tsp cayenne pepper (optional)
⅛ tsp ground cinnamon
⅛ tsp ground mace
⅛ tsp freshly ground pepper
1½ tsp ground cumin
1½ tsp salt (or a little more if needed)
8 tbsp plain yogurt
2 tbsp finely chopped fresh green coriander
2 medium-sized onions, peeled and coarsely chopped
3 cloves garlic, peeled and coarsely chopped

a piece of fresh ginger, about 2.5 cm (1 inch) cube, peeled and coarsely chopped
4 medium-sized eggs, hard boiled and peeled
6 tbsp vegetable oil
6 lightly crushed cardamom pods
2 bay leaves
2 whole dried hot red peppers (optional)
2 tsp ground turmeric
1 tsp paprika (for colour)
1 medium-sized tomato (tinned or fresh), peeled and finely chopped

---

If your butcher has not minced the meat 3 times, do it yourself at home. It should be *very* finely minced.

In a large bowl combine the meat, cloves, cayenne pepper, cinnamon, mace, black pepper, ½ tsp of the cumin, 1 tsp of the salt, 2 tbsp of the yogurt and the chopped green coriander. Mix well, cover bowl, and leave aside.

Place onion, garlic and ginger in container of an electric blender with 6 tbsp water and blend to a smooth paste.

Divide the minced meat into 4 portions. Wrap one portion around each peeled hard-boiled egg, covering it well.

Heat the vegetable oil in a 25–30 cm (10–12 inch) frying-pan over a medium-high flame, and put in the cardamom pods and bay leaves, and the red peppers if you want them. The spices will darken in a few seconds. Now put in the four meatballs and brown them all over. Turn them carefully so as not to break them. When they have browned, lift them out gently with a slotted spoon and place them on a plate.

To the same oil, add the paste from the blender container, keeping face averted, and fry, stirring, for about 10 minutes.

Now turn the flame to medium and add the coriander, the remaining 1 tsp cumin and the turmeric. Keep frying and stirring for a minute. Add 1 tbsp yogurt and stir for 1/2 minute. Add another tbsp yogurt and stir for 1/2 minute. Repeat this process until all the yogurt has been added. Now put in the remaining 1/2 tsp salt, the paprika, the chopped tomato and 175 ml (6 fl oz) water. Bring to the boil. Cover and simmer gently for 10 minutes.

Lift up lid and add the koftas. Cover and simmer gently for 1/2 hour. Turn the koftas every 7 or 8 minutes and spoon sauce over them.

To serve: Cut *koftas* in half and place on a warm platter. Spoon sauce over them and serve with almost any rice dish or with hot *chapatis*. Any yogurt *raita* and a pea or green bean dish would also go well with them.

Cubed lamb with onions and raisins

Serves 6–8

This dish is an adaptation I have made from *mullah do pyaza*, a Moghul favourite in which the meat is served with a lot of fried onions. These onions are cooked separately but are added to the meat for the last 5 minutes of cooking time. I brown the lamb pieces before I cook them, because, as I explained earlier, the meat in Britain seems to have a very high water content and will not brown with the spices, as it does in India.

1.4 kg (3 lb) boneless meat from shoulder of lamb, trimmed of excess fat, and cut into 2.5 cm (1 inch) cubes
11 tbsp vegetable oil
10 medium-sized onions
5 cloves garlic, peeled and coarsely chopped
a piece of fresh ginger, 5 cm (2 inches) long and 2.5 cm (1 inch) wide, peeled and coarsely chopped
1 tbsp ground coriander

2 tsp ground cumin
1 tsp ground turmeric
3 heaped tbsp plain yogurt
1 medium-sized tomato (tinned or fresh) peeled and finely chopped
1½ tsp salt
½ tsp ground cloves
½ tsp ground nutmeg
½ tsp ground cinnamon
1/8-1/4 tsp cayenne pepper (optional)
1/8 tsp freshly ground black pepper
2 tbsp golden seedless raisins

Dry the meat thoroughly with paper towels.

Heat 5 tbsp of oil in a wide, heavy-bottomed pot. When oil is very hot, fry 7 to 8 pieces of meat at a time, browning well on all sides, and then remove with a slotted spoon. When all the meat has browned, turn off the heat.

Peel and coarsely chop 2 of the onions and place them with the garlic, ginger and 5 tbsp of water in the container of an electric blender. Blend at high speed until you have a smooth paste.

Turn on the heat to medium under the pot in which you browned the meat. Pour in the paste from the blender and fry, stirring constantly, for about 5 minutes. Add the coriander, cumin and turmeric, and fry, stirring, for 1 minute. Add the yogurt, a tablespoon at a time, and keep stirring and frying. Then add the peeled and finely chopped tomato, and keep stirring. (In all, this should take about 10 minutes.) If after you have added the tomato some sticks to the bottom of your pot, add warm water, a teaspoon at a time, scraping the bottom and continuing to cook. The paste should turn a rich brown colour.

Put in the browned pieces of lamb along with any liquid that has accumulated, 300 ml (½ pint) of water, the salt, cloves, nutmeg, cinnamon, cayenne (if desired), and black pepper. Mix well. Bring to the boil. Cover, lower heat, and allow to simmer gently for 1 hour. (The beef should cook for 2½ hours.)

Meanwhile peel the other 8 onions, cut them in half lengthwise, and slice them into half-rings 3 mm (⅛ inch) thick.

Heat 3 tbsp of oil in each of two frying-pans over medium heat. (It is quicker and easier to use two frying-pans, frying half the onions in each simultaneously. You can also do them in two batches.) When the oil is hot, fry the onion slices for 10 to 12 minutes, until they are browned but not crisp. If the lamb has cooked for 55 minutes to an hour by this time, remove onions with a slotted spoon and add them to the meat. If not, remove with a slotted spoon to a bowl and set aside. Turn off the heat under one frying-pan. Into the other put the raisins and fry for a few seconds until they turn brown and puff up, then add to the meat pot if the meat is done or hold in the bowl with the fried onions. Once the onions and raisins have been added to the meat, simmer for 5 minutes.

To serve: Serve with pooris or chapatis, a yoghurt dish, a relish and a vegetable: cabbage or cauliflower would be good. Almost any plain rice or vegetable and rice dish can be served with it as well.

Lamb with onions and mushrooms, or lamb do pyaza

Serves 4–6

Any meat *do pyaza* usually means meat cooked with an equal weight of fried onions, *pyaz* being the North Indian word for onions. I have modified the traditional recipe slightly by adding mushrooms and by cooking with fenugreek, fennel and onion seeds instead of the more commonly used cardamom, cloves, peppercorns and cinnamon.

This is a mild-tasting dish, relatively easy to make and very popular with both children and adults.

---

900 g (2 lb) boned meat from shoulder of lamb, trimmed of excess fat, and cut into 2.5 cm (1 inch) cubes
5 medium-sized onions
vegetable oil (enough for 3 mm (1/8 inch) in bottom of frying-pan)
1/4 tsp whole black onion seeds (kalonji), if available

1/2 tsp whole fennel seeds
1/4 tsp whole cumin seeds
15 fenugreek seeds
100 ml (4 fl oz) plain yogurt
1 tsp salt (more if needed)
1/8 tsp freshly ground pepper
1/8–1/4 tsp cayenne pepper (optional)
225 g (8 oz) fresh mushrooms

Dry the meat thoroughly with paper towels and leave at room temperature while preparing the other ingredients.

Peel and halve the onions lengthwise. Slice them into 3 mm (1/8 inch) thick half-rings. In a 30 cm (12 inch) frying-pan heat the oil. Fry the onions over a high flame for 8 to 10 minutes, until they turn dark brown in spots and soften. Stir as you do this.

Remove onions with a slotted spoon and set aside in a bowl or dish.

In the same frying-pan put the onion seeds, fennel seeds, cumin seeds and fenugreek seeds. Within a few seconds the fennel seeds will begin to darken. As soon as this happens, put in the cubes of meat and fry for 5 to 10 minutes until well browned on all sides. While the meat is browning, put the yogurt in a bowl. Add 150 ml (1/4 pint) water to it very gradually, a tablespoon at a time, beating with a fork. Once the meat has browned, beat the yogurt mixture again and pour it into the frying-pan. Add salt, pepper and cayenne, bring to the boil, cover, lower heat to medium low, and cook for 25–35 minutes. Clean the mushrooms. Cut off the hard ends of the stems.

If the mushrooms are largish, quarter them whole (stem and all); if they are of medium size, halve them; if they are of button size, leave them whole. After the meat has cooked for 25 minutes, add the mushrooms. Stir well. Cover again and cook another for 25 minutes or until meat is tender.

Lift off the cover and add the fried onions. Raise heat to medium high and boil away most of the liquid. (The only 'sauce' should be what clings to the meat. At the bottom of the pan you should see just the fat.) This should take 5 minutes or less. Check the salt.

To serve: Here is an Indian dish that can be served as part of a traditional Indian dinner or as the main course of a Western-style meal.

At an Indian meal, you could serve it as we did very often on Sundays – with plain rice, Karhi and green beans.

Lamb (or beef) korma with almonds, pecans and sour cream

Serves 4–6

This dish can be made with shoulder or leg of lamb or stewing beef. Stewing beef generally takes much longer to cook, so adjust your time accordingly.

5 medium-sized onions

5 cloves garlic, peeled and coarsely chopped

a piece of fresh ginger, about 2.5 cm (1 inch) cube, peeled and coarsely chopped

vegetable oil, enough to have 1 mm ($^1/_{16}$ inch) in frying-pan

900 g (2 lb) boned meat from shoulder of lamb, trimmed of excess fat, and cut into 2.5–4 cm (1–1$^1/_2$ inch) cubes

1 tbsp ground coriander

2 tsp ground cumin

1 tsp ground turmeric

2 medium-sized tomatoes (tinned or fresh), peeled and finely chopped

$^1/_4$ tsp ground mace

$^1/_4$ tsp ground nutmeg

$^1/_4$ tsp ground cinnamon

$^1/_4$ tsp ground cloves

1 tsp salt (or as desired)

$^1/_8$ tsp freshly ground black pepper

$^1/_8$–$^1/_4$ tsp cayenne pepper (optional)

10 pecan halves

$^1/_4$ cup blanched almonds

2 tbsp sour cream

Garnish

5 cardamom pods

2 tbsp chopped fresh green coriander

the fried onions

Peel the onions. Cut 4 of them into halves lengthwise, and then slice them into very thin half-rings.

Chop the fifth onion coarsely. Put it along with the garlic and ginger in the container of an electric blender. Add 4 tbsp of water and blend at high speed until you have a smooth paste.

Heat oil in a 25–30 cm (10–12 inch) frying-pan (use a deep, heavy-bottomed frying-pan with lid or a wide casserole-type dish) over medium-high heat. Put in the sliced onions and fry, stirring, for 15 to 20 minutes or until they are dark brown and crisp, not black and burned. Remove them with a slotted spoon and spread on paper towels to drain. (You will not need them until serving time.)

Dry the pieces of meat thoroughly and brown them well, about 8 pieces at a time, in the onion-flavoured oil. As each batch gets done, remove with slotted spoon to a platter. When all the meat is browned, turn off the heat.

When the frying-pan has cooled a bit, pour in the paste from the electric blender. Stir it well, mixing it with the coagulated pan juices. Turn the heat on medium high and fry the paste, stirring all the time, for 8 to 10 minutes, or until it has browned. Now lower heat and add the coriander, cumin and turmeric. Mix and fry, stirring for a minute or two. Add the chopped tomatoes and fry another minute.

Next add the mace, nutmeg, cinnamon and cloves. Mix and cook slowly for 5 minutes. Stir every now and then.

Now add 150 ml (1/4 pint) water, the salt, black pepper, cayenne pepper and browned meat, as well as the juices that have accumulated. Bring to the boil, cover, lower heat and simmer gently for 30 minutes.

If you want to remove the fat, skim it off as it rises to the top.

Put the pecans and almonds in a blender with 3 tbsp of water, and blend at high speed until you have a smooth paste. You may need to stop and push down with a rubber spatula a few times.

Add the nut paste, then the sour cream, to the meat. Stir and check the salt. Bring to the boil, cover, lower heat, and simmer gently for 25 to 30 minutes or until meat is tender.

Peel the cardamoms, discarding the skin. Crush the seeds with a heavy mortar and pestle or put them through a clean pepper grinder.

To serve: Place the meat and gravy in a wide bowl. Garnish with ground cardamom seeds, chopped green coriander and the fried onions. Serve with hot chapatis or parathas, or almost any rice dish. Cabbage, green beans, and carrot dishes would go well with this korma. For a relish, choose something with raw onions and tomato.

Lamb cooked in dark almond sauce (badami roghan josh)

Serves 4-6

Roghan josh is a traditional North Indian Muslim dish. It has a thick, dark, nutty sauce made with almonds and roasted cumin, coriander and coconut. Even though shoulder of lamb is used here, you could use leg, neck or shank. Stewing beef may also be substituted.

900 g (2 lb) boned meat from shoulder of lamb, cubed into 2.5 cm (1 inch) pieces
6 tbsp vegetable oil
10 whole cloves
1–2 whole dried hot red peppers (optional)
12 peppercorns
6 whole cardamom pods
1 tbsp ground cumin
2 tbsp ground coriander
1 tbsp desiccated unsweetened coconut
3 tbsp blanched almonds, coarsely chopped

6 cloves garlic, peeled and coarsely chopped
a piece of fresh ginger, about 2.5 cm (1 inch) cube, peeled and coarsely chopped
1/2 tsp ground turmeric
1/4 tsp ground nutmeg
1/4 tsp ground mace
2 medium-sized onions, peeled and finely minced
3 tbsp plain yogurt
3 medium-sized tomatoes (tinned or fresh), peeled and coarsely chopped
1 1/2 tsp salt

Wipe the meat well with paper towels.

Heat the oil in a 25–30 cm (10–12 inch) frying-pan. When the oil is hot, add the cloves, red peppers, peppercorns, and cardamom. Stir them for a few seconds until they puff up and darken.

Now put in 7 or 8 pieces of meat at a time to brown. When each lot is brown on all sides, remove with a slotted spoon to a large flameproof covered casserole, taking care to leave the spices in the frying-pan. Continue to brown all the meat this way and set aside. Turn off flame under frying-pan.

You have to roast some spices now, so take out your heaviest iron-type frying-pan (I keep a small one just for this purpose). Put the cumin, coriander, coconut and almonds in it. Turn heat to medium and roast, stirring, for about 5 minutes or until spices turn a coffee colour. Turn off heat and pour roasted spices and nuts into container of electric blender. Add chopped garlic and ginger.

With a slotted spoon, lift out the fried spices in the oil and put them in the blender container too. Add the turmeric, nutmeg, mace and 8 tbsp water. Blend at high speed until you have a smooth, thick paste. You may need to stop the blender and push down with a rubber spatula.

In the same frying-pan in which the lamb cooked, fry the onions over high heat, stirring and scraping up the juices for about 5 minutes, or until they turn dark in spots. Then lower heat to medium and add paste from blender. Stir and fry for another 5 minutes, gradually adding the yogurt, a tablespoon at a time. Put in the chopped tomatoes. Stir and fry another 2–3 minutes.

Now add 300 ml (1/2 pint) water. Bring to the boil. Cover, lower heat, and simmer gently for 15 minutes.

Put the meat into this sauce. Add the salt and stir. Bring to the boil, cover, lower heat, and simmer gently for 1 hour. Stir a few times as it cooks.

To serve: Place in a warm dish, cover, and take to the table. Roghan Josh goes very well with pooris or chapatis and Rice with Spinach. Serve a yogurt dish with it, and cauliflower or carrots.

Lamb with spinach

Serves 6–8

This is a traditional Moghul recipe. I use lamb for the recipe, but you could use beef (chuck or round) if you like.

1.4 kg (3 lb) fresh spinach (or three 340 g (12 oz) packages of frozen spinach)

3 medium-sized onions, peeled and coarsely chopped

a piece of fresh ginger, 5 cm (2 inches) long and 2.5 cm (1 inch) wide, peeled and coarsely chopped

7–8 cloves garlic, peeled and coarsely chopped

1 fresh hot green chilli, chopped (optional), or 1/8–1/2 tsp cayenne pepper

8 tbsp vegetable oil

1.4 kg (3 lb) boneless meat from shoulder of lamb, cut into 2.5 cm

(1 inch) cubes (or shank, neck, or leg – see page 39 for proportions)

1 cinnamon stick, 7.5 cm (3 inches) long

7 whole cloves

7 whole cardamom pods

2 bay leaves

2 tbsp ground coriander

1 tbsp ground cumin

1 tsp ground turmeric

1 medium-sized tomato (tinned or fresh), peeled and finely chopped

2 tbsp plain yogurt

1 1/2 tsp salt

1 tbsp garam masala

In a large pot, bring about 4.5 litres (8 pints) of water to boil. Meanwhile, trim and wash the fresh spinach thoroughly in cold water. Make sure you get all the sand out.

Drop the spinach in the boiling water, a third at a time, and let it boil until the leaves wilt. You may need to push it down occasionally. As each batch wilts, scoop it out into a colander and run cold water over it. (If you are using frozen spinach, cook according to directions and drain.) When all the spinach is done, squeeze out most of the water and mince it. Keep aside in bowl.

Place the chopped onions, chopped ginger, garlic, green chilli and 5 tbsp of water in the blender container and blend at high speed until you have a smooth paste (about 1 minute).

Heat the oil in a 4.5–5.7 litre (8–10 pint) heavy-bottomed pot over medium heat. Pat dry the cubes of meat thoroughly on paper towels. Put 7 or 8 pieces at a time into the hot oil and brown them on all sides. Remove with a slotted spoon and set aside.

Put the cinnamon stick, cloves, cardamom pods and bay leaves in the same hot oil. Stir. When the bay leaves begin to darken (10 to 20 seconds), add the paste from the blender (keep face averted). Keep stirring and frying for 10 minutes until the mixture darkens (if it sticks to the bottom, sprinkle a teaspoon of water at a time, and keep frying).

Now lower the flame and, continuing to stir and fry constantly, add at intervals first the coriander, cumin and turmeric, 2 minutes later the chopped tomato, then about 5 minutes later the yogurt, and finally 2 minutes later the browned meat cubes. When meat and spices are well mixed put in the spinach. Add salt, bring to the boil, then cover and lower the heat to allow the mixture to simmer gently for 50 minutes. (Most meat gives out enough water for it to cook in its own juice, as it were. If you find that the meat is sticking, you can add up to 150 ml (¼ pint) of warm water.) Stir occasionally as it cooks.

At the end of the cooking time, uncover, increase heat, and cook rapidly until most of the liquid evaporates, leaving a thick sauce. Put in the *garam masala* and stir gently, being careful not to break meat pieces.

To serve: Place in warm dish and serve with chapatis, Potatoes with Asafetida and Cumin and Yogurt with Roasted Courgettes. Or you could serve it with plain boiled rice, and lentils, and a cauliflower dish if you like.

Sindhi gosht (Sindhi meat)

Serves 6

The meat (lamb) is marinated for 3 to 4 hours in a paste of onions, garlic, ginger, coriander, cumin, turmeric, red pepper, salt, pepper and vinegar. It is then cooked in this marinade, with the addition of onion and fennel seeds.

1.25 kg (2½ lb) boneless meat from lamb shoulder, cut into 2.5 cm (1 inch) cubes
2 medium-sized onions, peeled and coarsely chopped
a piece of fresh ginger, 5 cm (2 inches) long and 2.5 cm (1 inch) wide, coarsely chopped
6 cloves garlic, peeled and coarsely chopped
1 tbsp ground coriander

2 tsp ground cumin
1 tsp ground turmeric
⅛–½ tsp cayenne pepper (optional; use desired amount)
100 ml (4 fl oz) red wine vinegar
1 tsp salt
2 tsp whole fennel seeds
1 tsp whole black onion seeds (kalonji), if available
5 tbsp vegetable oil

Remove fat and tissue from the cubes of meat.

In the container of an electric blender, place the chopped onions, ginger, garlic, coriander, cumin, turmeric, cayenne pepper (if used), vinegar and salt. Blend at high speed until you have a smooth paste.

Pour paste into a bowl large enough to contain the meat. Prick the meat with a fork or with the point of a sharp knife and place in marinade. Mix well, cover, and leave for 3 to 4 hours. (Refrigerate if it is a very hot day; otherwise leave at room temperature.)

After the meat has marinated, pour contents of bowl into a wide 4.5 litre (8 pint) cooking pot. Add the fennel and onion seeds. Bring to the boil. Cover, lower heat, and simmer about 1 hour.

Lift off cover. Taste to check the salt (you may want to add a little more). Raise the heat and boil rapidly until most of the liquid evaporates. You will need to stir more frequently as the liquid diminishes. Now add the oil and keep stirring and frying over a medium flame. The dish must be 'dry', i.e. a thickish sauce should cling to the meat, which browns as the liquid cooks down. Be careful not to break meat pieces as you stir.

To serve: Place in a warmed dish and serve with chapatis, parathas, or pooris. You could also serve it with almost any kind of rice. With it, serve peas, okra, beans or cabbage, and some yogurt dish.

Lamb chops with whole spices and yogurt

Serves 4

In this dish, lamb chops are cooked with whole spices, garlic, ginger, green coriander and yogurt. It is simple to make and very delicious in its final blend of flavours.

---

8 lamb chops
4 heaped tbsp plain yogurt
3 tbsp vegetable oil
10 whole black peppercorns
10 whole cloves
2 bay leaves
8 cardamom pods
2 cinnamon sticks, 5 cm (2 inches) long

2 whole dried hot red peppers (optional)
a piece of fresh ginger, about 2.5 cm (1 inch) cube, peeled and minced
2 cloves garlic, peeled and minced
4 tbsp chopped fresh green coriander, or use fresh mint, watercress, or regular parsley as a substitute
1 tsp salt

Trim lamb chops of excess fat, leaving 3 mm (1/8 inch) along the sides. Pat dry with paper towels.

Mix the yogurt with 250 ml (8 fl oz) of water and set aside in a non-metallic bowl.

Heat the oil in a 25–30 cm (10–12 inch) heavy-bottomed pot. When oil is very hot, put in 4 chops at a time, brown well on both sides, and remove with slotted spoon. Turn heat down to medium and fry the whole spices (peppercorns, cloves, bay leaves, cardamom, cinnamon and red peppers) for about 20 seconds or until the bay leaves turn darker. Now add minced ginger and garlic, and fry, stirring, for a minute. Add the coriander and keep stirring for another minute.

Now put lamb chops back into the pot along with any liquid that may have collected in the bowl. Stir the yogurt water once again and pour over chops. Add salt, bring to the boil, cover, and simmer one hour. Stir gently every 10 minutes.

To Serve: Serve with Rice with Peas, Cucumber Raita, and any of the green bean recipes. Or serve with plain boiled potatoes and a green salad.

'Butterflied' leg of lamb, marinated and barbecued

Serves 10–12

This is, quite easily, one of my favourite meat dishes. I ask the butcher to 'butterfly' a 3.6–4 kg (8–9 lb) leg of lamb for me. The 'butterflying' process involves boning the leg in such a manner that the whole piece of meat lies flat, rather like a large, uneven steak. I then marinate it for 24 hours in olive oil, lemon juice, and a paste of onions, garlic, ginger, coriander, cumin, turmeric, mace, nutmeg, cloves, cinnamon, black pepper, cayenne pepper, garam masala, salt and an orange food colouring which gives it the orange look that traditional tandoori meats have. After it is well marinated, it is best grilled outdoors on charcoal, though you could do it in your indoor grill – with less spectacular results! It is excellent to take along on picnics (pack the meat in a couple of plastic bags and the marinade in a tight jar – take along a pastry brush for brushing on the thick marinade paste), and refrigerated left-overs taste superb the next day. It is difficult to describe the 'style' this meat is cooked in. It is perhaps a combination of the tandoori school, my sister Kamal's lamb chops, and our Indian cook's roast mutton.

---

1 leg of lamb, 3.6–4 kg (8–9 lb), butterflied

2 medium-sized onions (1 coarsely chopped, 1 for garnishing)

a piece of fresh ginger, 7.5 cm (3 inches) long and 2.5 cm (1 inch) wide, peeled and coarsely chopped

5–7 cloves garlic (depending on preference – I use 7), peeled and coarsely chopped

175 ml (6 fl oz) lemon juice

1 tbsp ground coriander

1 tsp ground cumin

1 tsp garam masala

1 tsp ground turmeric

1/4 tsp ground mace

1/4 tsp ground nutmeg

1/4 tsp ground cinnamon

1/4 tsp ground cloves

250 ml (8 fl oz) olive oil

2 1/2 tsp salt

1/4 tsp freshly ground pepper

1/2–1 tsp cayenne pepper (optional – use less if you like, or none)

2 tsp orange food colouring (Spanish bijol, or Indian food colouring obtainable in powdered form, or Bush's orange-red powder)

Garnish

12 radishes

Put the chopped onion, ginger, garlic and 4 tbsp of the lemon juice in the container of the electric blender, and blend at high speed to get a smooth paste (about 1 minute).

In a bowl or a pot with a non-metallic lining, large enough to hold the meat, put the paste from the blender and all the other ingredients except the meat and the onion and radishes to be used for garnishing later. Mix well.

Carefully cut off all fat and tissue from the meat, and with the point of a knife make lots of jabs in it on both sides. Put the meat in the marinade paste. Fold the meat over, or cut it into 2 pieces, if there is not room. Make a few more jabs with the knife, and be sure the paste gets rubbed into the meat and goes way inside the gashes. Cover the container and leave refrigerated for 24 hours. Turn the meat over at least 3 or 4 times during this period.

The meat is now ready for grilling. But before you start, get your garnishes ready.

Peel the second onion and slice it into very fine rounds (paper-thin if possible). Separate the rounds into rings and put them into a bowl of ice water, cover, and refrigerate.

Cut off the stems, leaves and tips from the radishes and then cut them into flowers. (Starting from the tip end, start cutting into halves, but stop short as you reach the stem end. Next, cut into quarters and eighths the same way.) Put into a small bowl of ice water, cover, and refrigerate. It will look prettier if you use unblemished radishes of approximately the same size for this.

Now light your fire. If it takes 20 to 30 minutes to get red hot, start about 1 hour and 15 minutes before you intend to eat. When hot, place the metal grill at the lowest notch.

Lift meat from bowl (leaving marinade) and place on grill. Sear 5 to 8 minutes (depending on your stove) on either side. Now raise the grill to its topmost notch and cook about 20 minutes on each side. Brush frequently with the marinade until it is all used up. If you don't have a grill that moves up and down, just remember that the meat needs to cook about 50 minutes and it should be very dark on the outside and pinkish inside. Most Indians like their meat well done; you may prefer it a bit rare, but don't cook it too rare, as the spices inside won't get a chance to cook through.

To serve: Warm a large platter. Meanwhile place the meat on a carving board and cut it into thin slices. Use a very sharp knife, and do this as fast as you can, as you don't want the meat to cool off too much. Now slide the meat pieces onto the warm platter, leaving the slices in roughly the same shape as the piece of meat. Drain off the water from the radishes and onion rings. Arrange radishes around meat and lay raw onion rings on top of meat. Serve immediately.

Boti kabab (cubed lamb kabab)

Serves 6

In this recipe, cubed lamb pieces are marinated overnight in a blend of yogurt, tomato purée, dry mustard, oil, lemon juice, garlic, ginger, turmeric and a host of other spices. The next day, they are skewered and grilled over charcoal. The meat must cook slowly, as it needs to cook through. Also, nothing tastes worse than uncooked turmeric! (You could make this same recipe in a gas or electric grill.) Keep the meat about 10 cm (4 inches) from heat and cook 7 to 10 minutes on each side or until each side is well browned, depending on the heat of the grill. It should not be too rare inside or the spices will taste uncooked.

3 tbsp tomato purée
6 tbsp plain yogurt
2 tsp dry English mustard
2 tsp salt
150 ml (1/4 pint) olive oil
   (or vegetable oil)
4 tbsp lemon juice
1 tbsp ground coriander
1 tbsp ground cumin
1 tbsp ground turmeric
1 tbsp garam masala
1/2 tsp ground cloves
1/2 tsp ground mace
1/2 tsp ground nutmeg

1/2 tsp ground cinnamon
10 cloves garlic, peeled and
   coarsely chopped
a piece of ginger, 2.5 cm (1 inch)
   square, peeled and coarsely
   chopped
1/4–1 tsp cayenne pepper (optional,
   or use as desired)
1.25 kg (2 1/2 lb) meat from leg of
   lamb, cut into 2.5 cm (1 inch)
   cubes

Garnish
1 medium-sized onion

In the container of an electric blender, place the tomato purée, yogurt, mustard, salt, 50 ml (2 fl oz) of the olive oil, lemon juice, coriander, cumin, turmeric, garam masala, cloves, mace, nutmeg, cinnamon, garlic, ginger and cayenne. Blend marinade paste at high speed until all the spices are well mixed and the ginger and garlic have puréed (about 1 minute).

Remove all the fat from the meat pieces. Stab pieces with the point of a sharp knife, then place them in a glass or ceramic bowl. Pour the marinade over the meat. Mix well, cover, and refrigerate at least 4 hours but preferably overnight.

The meat will take 30 to 40 minutes to cook, so light your charcoal fire or preheat your grill accordingly. String the meat cubes loosely on several skewers. If you crowd them too tightly, adjacent sides of the cubes will not brown. Arrange the grill so that it is not too close to the flame, 10–12 cm (4–5 inches away). Place skewers on grill and cook each side for 7 to 10 minutes or until it is nicely browned. Baste frequently with remaining olive oil. When all sides are browned, remove meat from skewers and place on warm platter.

To serve: Peel the onion and slice into *very* fine rings, paper-thin if possible. Separate the rings and place them on top of meat. Serve simply with green salad and boiled potatoes. (A good idea is to boil the potatoes ahead of time and then, when you begin your grilling, peel the potatoes, rub them with oil and some of the marinade paste, and grill them along with the meat for about 20 minutes, turning them as they brown.) This meat could also be served with Rice with Spinach.

Pork chops cooked with whole spices and tamarind juice

Serves 4

Indians sometimes use Western cuts of meat to cook local dishes. We did not eat pork very often in our home, but every now and then my father would drive down to a special butcher to buy pork chops. Here is one of the ways we ate them. N.B. This dish should be cooked in a stainless steel pan or a pan lined with porcelain, enamel or teflon.

---

1 tamarind lump about the size of a walnut
8 loin or rib pork chops
2 tbsp vegetable oil
12 whole black peppercorns
10 whole cloves
2 cinnamon sticks, each 6.5 cm (2½ inches) long

8 whole cardamom pods
2 cloves of garlic, peeled
2 whole dried hot red peppers (optional)
1½ tsp salt
1 tsp granulated sugar

Soak the tamarind lump in 175 ml (6 fl oz) hot water for at least 2 hours. Pat dry the eight pork chops with paper towels. Trim off all but 3 mm (¹/8 inch) fat along the sides.

Heat oil in a 25–30 cm (10–12 inch) heavy-bottomed pot over medium-high heat. When oil is very hot, put in 4 pork chops at a time and brown them on both sides. This should take 3 to 4 minutes on each side.

Once the pork chops have browned, remove them to a side dish and keep covered. Lower flame to medium.

In the same oil place first the peppercorns, then the cloves, the cinnamon, the cardamom pods, the garlic and finally the red pepper. Stir and fry these ingredients for about a minute or less until the red peppers darken and the garlic is a bit browned.

Now return the pork chops to the frying-pan and add 300 ml (½ pint) warm water and 1 tsp salt. Bring to the boil, cover, lower heat, and allow to cook very gently for ½ hour. Turn the chops over a few times as they cook.

Meanwhile, press the tamarind juice and pulp through a strainer into a non-metallic bowl. Discard tamarind fibres, skins, seeds, etc.

When the pork chops have cooked for 30 minutes, add 2 tbsp tamarind juice, 1 tsp sugar and ½ tsp salt. Mix well, turning the chops. Cover and keep cooking slowly another 20 to 30 minutes. By this time most of the liquid will have been absorbed, leaving just the fat behind.

To serve: In India, the fat and the spices would be served with the meat. Here, in Britain, I suggest you lift the chops from the pot with a slotted spoon, leaving all the oil and spices behind.

Place on a warm platter and serve with Rice with Peas or any other vegetable rice dish. For a vegetable, the Cabbage with Onions would be a good idea. If you are not up to cooking a complicated vegetable dish (as I am sometimes not), serve just a salad, or sliced tomatoes.

Pork chops à la Jaffrey

Serves 2

I apologize for this name. The dish is really my very own concoction and unlikely to be served in any Indian home other than mine. Indians almost never use celery in their cooking. Nor do they often use soy sauce, though I must say that in the major cities the influence of an overcooked version of Chinese cuisine is certainly making itself felt. This recipe acknowledges its debt to that cuisine, but tastes, in the last analysis, rather Indian.

---

4 pork chops (loin or rib)
2 tbsp vegetable oil
2 bay leaves
1 hot dried red pepper (optional)
8 whole cloves
1 large stick of celery, diced
1 medium-sized onion, coarsely
   chopped

a piece of fresh ginger, 2.5 cm
   (1 inch) long and 1 cm
   (½ inch) wide, sliced into
   3 rounds
2 cloves garlic, peeled
⅛ tsp ground cinnamon
⅛ tsp ground mace
3 tbsp soy sauce
1½ tsp granulated sugar
½ lemon

Try to get pork chops that are evenly cut, so that they may brown evenly. Pat the chops dry and trim all but 0.5 cm (¼ inch) of the fat. Place them in a large frying-pan and turn heat on high. The chops should brown in their own fat. When they are a golden colour on both sides (press down areas that refuse to touch the frying-pan), remove them from frying-pan and place in bowl or plate. Turn off the heat and pour off only the accumulated fat in the frying-pan.

Heat the vegetable oil along with the coagulated juices in the same frying-pan over a medium flame, and put in the bay leaves, red pepper and cloves. Stir. When the bay leaves change colour (this should take a few seconds) add celery, onions, ginger and garlic. Stirring, fry over medium flame for 4 to 5 minutes or until everything is slightly browned. Add the browned pork chops, cinnamon, mace, soy sauce, sugar and 50 ml (2 fl oz) water. Cut the lemon into 4 round slices (skin and all – remove pips though) and place over chops. Bring to the boil. Cover, lower heat, and simmer gently 50 minutes to 1 hour or until tender. Turn and mix gently every 10 to 15 minutes.

To serve: Place contents of frying-pan on platter and serve with Plain Basmati Rice and a green salad. A yogurt type of relish would be a good side dish. If you like you can remove the pieces of ginger and garlic before you serve.

Sweetbreads with fresh green coriander

Serves 6

900 g (2 lb) sweetbreads
2 medium-sized onions
4 cloves garlic, peeled and coarsely
    chopped
a piece of fresh ginger, 6.5 cm
    (2½ inches) long and 2.5 cm
    (1 inch) wide, peeled and
    coarsely chopped
5 tbsp vegetable oil
1 hot green chilli, finely sliced
    (more or less as desired), or
    ⅛–½ tsp cayenne pepper
    (as desired)

4 tbsp chopped fresh green
    coriander
2 tsp ground coriander
1 tsp ground cumin
½ tsp ground turmeric
1 medium-sized tomato (tinned or
    fresh), peeled and finely chopped
2 tbsp plain yogurt
1¾ tsp salt
2 tbsp white vinegar
1 tbsp lemon juice

Soak the sweetbreads in ice water for 1 hour.

Meanwhile, peel the onions. Slice one into fine rings and halve the rings. Set aside. Chop the other onion coarsely.

Put the chopped onion, garlic and ginger in container of electric blender, add 3 tbsp of water, and blend at high speed until you have a smooth paste (about 1 minute). Leave in container.

Heat the oil in a 25–30 cm (10–12 inch) frying-pan over medium heat. When hot, put in the halved onion rings and fry them, stirring, for about 5 minutes until they are crisp, dark brown, but not burned. With a slotted spoon, remove them and spread on paper towels.

Pour the paste from blender into the onion-flavoured oil. Fry, stirring, for 6 to 8 minutes, or until mixture turns a medium golden-brown. Add at intervals, stirring continuously, the green chilli (or cayenne) and the green coriander; then, after 1 minute, lower the flame and add the coriander, cumin, turmeric; after another minute, the chopped tomato; and then the yogurt, continuing to fry and stir, for 2 to 3 minutes; finally ³/₄ tsp salt and 4 tbsp warm water. Bring to the boil, cover, lower heat, and allow the mixture to simmer for 15 minutes.

In a large pot, bring 3.4 litres (6 pints) of water to boil. Add 1 tsp salt and the vinegar. Remove the sweetbreads from the ice water and drain. Plunge them into the boiling water, drain, and plunge again into the ice water. Remove connecting tissue carefully (you can almost peel it off) and break sweetbreads into 2.5–4 cm (1–1¹/₂ inch) pieces.

After the sauce has cooked for about 15 minutes, add the sweetbread pieces and lemon juice; stir, cover again, and cook gently for another 15 minutes.

To serve: Place in a warm dish. Sprinkle with the browned onions, and serve with hot chapatis and a vegetable and a yogurt dish of your choice. You could also serve any tomato or onion relish.

POULTRY

Until a few years ago there were only two ways one could buy poultry in India. Either you went up to the poultry market where live birds were kept in coops and you selected one, or you would wait at home for the poultry man to come around, hawking his wares. If he was somewhat affluent, he would arrive on a bicycle, but more often than not he came at a half-run, on his own two feet. On his humped shoulders he carried a bamboo, bent by the weight of a large basket dangling at each end. The lower section of these baskets was wicker, while the top was made of a rope mesh which could be opened and closed like an old-fashioned pouch. The occupants of these swaying baskets were the indignant birds – chickens and ducks mostly - which could not be seen except for a head here, a foot there, and a tail sticking out of the rope mesh; but they could be heard from a distance, squawking, quacking and cackling. One had to know how to pick a bird by feeling its flesh. Experts like my father could even tell the age of the bird by prodding and squeezing in the right places.

In the last few years refrigeration and freezing have increased tremendously. The result is that poultry farms have mushroomed all over the country. The birds are sent, cleaned and plucked, to speciality stores where they can be bought much as they are in Britain. Of course, this is true only of the larger cities. The small towns and villages still rely on the old system.

The chickens in India seem to me to have more flavour than chickens here, though they can frequently be fairly tough, requiring a much longer cooking time. The only chicken that can be grilled in India is the 675 g–1.25 kg (1½–2½ lb) spring chicken, and even then the bird must first be tenderized in a marinade containing green papaya or yogurt.

The Moghul miniature painters of the seventeenth century often showed royalty at the hunt, the *shikar*. Seated on cushioned, throne-like howdahs atop elephants or camels, they hunted anything from tigers to quail. The *shikar* still goes on, and although big game is generally left to the very rich, duck, geese, partridge and quail can still be had by the ordinary Mr Singh on the street. Many restaurants have partridges on their daily menu, and many homes, like mine, serve roast duck frequently during the winter season.

The chicken available in British markets is so tender that it begins to fall apart well before it can go through the several stages required in most Indian recipes. Very often the chicken is cooked before the spices have permeated the meat. I have tried to adjust the chicken recipes to the tenderness of the English supermarket birds.

Most Indian chicken recipes require the removal of the skin before the bird is cooked. My English butcher shakes his head in despair every time I request this. To spare his feelings, I have now taken to doing the task myself. It is really quite easy and can be accomplished with a sharp, point-ed knife and a bit of tugging in certain places.

Also, Indians generally cut their chicken into small pieces but rarely remove the bones. Legs are separated into drumsticks and thighs, breasts are cut into four or six pieces, backs into two or three, and wings into two. The reason is to allow the spices to penetrate the meat and bones as much as possible. I often serve just legs and breasts. They are easier to handle with knife and fork, and no one is stuck with the back. Backs and wings necessitate digital manipulation. They are to be avoided if you have finicky eaters.

While chicken is considered rather ordinary fare in this country, in India it is still regarded as an indulgence reserved for the rich. To be served chicken in someone's house definitely means that you are getting special treatment. In restaurants it is always one of the more expensive items on the menu.

In my recipes you will notice that I often brown the chicken quickly before I leave it to cook. In India this browning is done either with the paste of onions, garlic, ginger and spices or at the end, when the chicken is cooked and the sauce has been reduced over high heat. Since the bird cooks very quickly here, any attempt at browning during these two stages leaves my chicken a disintegrated, shattered mess. I have discovered that an initial browning of the chicken provides the right colour and the bird does not fall apart.

Chicken cooked with yogurt

Serves 4–6

Here is a simple chicken recipe using very few of the spices generally associated with Indian cuisine. Yet the dish is typically North Indian. It is easy to make and very popular with children and adults alike.

---

4 chicken legs
1 whole chicken breast
150 ml (¼ pint) plus 2 tbsp plain
   yogurt
5 medium-sized onions
2 cloves garlic, peeled and coarsely
   chopped

a piece of fresh ginger, about 2.5 cm
   (1 inch) cube, peeled and
   coarsely chopped
7 tbsp vegetable oil
1 tsp salt
⅛–¼ tsp cayenne pepper (as and if
   desired)

Skin all the chicken pieces. Divide each leg into 2 pieces (drumstick and thigh). Quarter the chicken breast. Pat dry the chicken pieces and set aside.

Put 150 ml (¼ pint) yogurt in a bowl. Add 175 ml (6 fl oz) water, a little at a time, beating with a fork as you do so.

Peel all the onions. Cut 4 in half, lengthwise, then slice them into half-rings, about 3 mm (⅛ inch) thick. Chop the other onion coarsely.

Put the chopped onion, garlic and ginger in the container of an electric blender. Add 6 tbsp of water and blend to a smooth paste.

Heat 5 tbsp of the oil in a 25 cm (10 inch) pot over medium heat. Put in the sliced onions and fry them, stirring, for 8 to 10 minutes or until they have turned dark brown at the edges but are still limp. Remove them with a slotted spoon to a small bowl and set aside.

Add the remaining 2 tbsp of oil to the pot and put in about 4 pieces of chicken at a time. Fry them, at medium-high heat, for 7 to 8 minutes or until they are browned on all sides. Remove chicken pieces to plate with a slotted spoon.

Turn heat to low and pour paste from the blender into the pot, keeping your face averted. Scrape the bottom of the pot for browned meat juices and mix in scrapings with the paste. Now raise the heat to medium and fry, stirring, for 4 to 5 minutes. Add 1 tbsp plain yogurt, scraping bottom of pot and continuing to fry and stir for another minute. Then add 1 more tbsp yogurt, stirring for another minute.

Now put into the pot the chicken pieces, the well-blended yogurt and water mixture, the salt and the cayenne pepper (if you desire it). Stir and bring to the boil. Cover, lower heat, and simmer 20 minutes.

Remove lid, raise heat to medium, and cook for 5 minutes to boil down some of the liquid, turning the chicken pieces carefully. (You should be left with a thick sauce.)

Mix in reserved fried onions, and cook at same heat for another 2 minutes, stirring occasionally.

To serve: Place contents of pot in warmed dish and serve with hot pooris or hot chapatis or almost any kind of rice. You might serve okra or aubergine or green beans as a vegetable. Since this dish is cooked with yogurt, serve a non-yogurt relish, such as Cucumber and Tomato with Lemon Juice. A fresh green chutney (mint or coriander) might also be refreshing.

Chicken with potatoes

Serves 2–3

---

3 medium-sized potatoes for boiling
1 medium-sized onion, peeled and
    coarsely chopped
3 cloves garlic, peeled and coarsely
    chopped
a piece of fresh ginger, about
    2.5 cm (1 inch) cube, peeled and
    coarsely chopped
675 g (1½ lb) chicken sections
5 tbsp vegetable oil
1 cinnamon stick, 6.5–7.5 cm
    (2½–3 inches) long

1 bay leaf
4 whole cardamom pods
2 whole hot dried red peppers
    (optional)
2 whole black peppercorns
½ tsp ground turmeric
1 tbsp tomato purée
600 ml (1 pint) chicken broth (tinned
    or homemade)
½ tsp salt

Put your potatoes on to boil. When done, drain off water and leave potatoes to cool. (Do not use boiled potatoes which have been refrigerated for this recipe.)

Place onion, garlic and ginger in container of blender with 5 tbsp water and blend to smooth paste.

Remove skin from chicken pieces and pat them dry.

Heat oil in a 30 cm (12 inch) frying-pan over medium-high flame, then add the cinnamon, bay leaf, cardamom, red peppers, peppercorns and chicken pieces. Fry chicken pieces quickly on all sides until golden-brown. Remove chicken with slotted spoon and set aside.

Pour the paste from blender into frying-pan, averting your face. Add turmeric and fry, stirring, for about 3 minutes. Now add the tomato purée and the chicken broth. Mix. Bring to the boil. Cover, lower heat, and simmer gently for 15 minutes.

Peel and quarter the potatoes. Add salt, the browned chicken pieces and the potatoes to the sauce. Stir, bring to the boil, cover, lower heat, and simmer gently for 20 to 25 minutes or until chicken is tender. Turn chicken and potatoes a few times while they are cooking.

To serve: Put chicken pieces, potatoes, and sauce into a bowl and serve with hot chapatis, parathas, or pooris. Serve green beans or peas with it and at least one kind of relish (a yogurt relish might be a good idea).

Chicken with sliced lemon and fried onions

Serves 4–6

Cooked with lemon slices, sugar and fried onions, this chicken dish is unusual and quite delicious. You could use a whole bird, cut into small sections, or you could buy just legs and breasts, dividing the legs into drumstick and thigh and quartering the breast.

N.B. This dish should be cooked in a stainless steel pot or a pot lined with porcelain, enamel or teflon.

1.4–1.6 kg (3–3½ lb) chicken sections	½ tsp ground turmeric
3 medium-sized onions	2 tbsp plain yogurt
a piece of fresh ginger, about 2.5 cm (1 inch) cube, peeled and coarsely chopped	1 tbsp tomato purée
	1 tsp salt
4 cloves garlic, peeled and coarsely chopped	¼ tsp ground cinnamon
	¼ tsp ground cloves
8 tbsp vegetable oil	⅛ tsp cayenne pepper
1 tbsp ground coriander	1 whole lemon
1 tsp ground cumin	1 tbsp sugar
	⅛ tsp freshly ground pepper

Skin all the chicken pieces and pat them dry.

Peel the onions. Chop two of them coarsely and put them into the container of an electric blender. Cut the third one in half lengthwise, then slice it into thin half-rounds and set aside.

Add 6 tbsp of water, the ginger and the garlic to the onions in the blender and blend at high speed until you have a smooth paste.

Heat 6 tbsp of the oil in a 25–30 cm (10–12 inch) pot over medium-high flame. When hot, put in the sliced onions and fry them, stirring, until they are darkish brown and crisp, though not burned. Remove onions with a slotted spoon and leave them to drain on paper towels.

In the same oil, brown the chicken pieces on all sides until they are golden. (Do this speedily over high flame so chicken browns but does not cook through. You will need to do it in at least two batches.) Remove chicken with slotted spoon to a bowl or plate.

Add the remaining 2 tbsp of oil to the pot. Pour in the paste from the blender. (Keep face averted.) Stirring, fry on medium-high heat for about 10 minutes or until paste turns a nice golden-brown. Now put in the coriander, cumin and turmeric and fry, stirring continuously; after another 2 minutes add yogurt, a teaspoon at a time; after 2 or 3 minutes, the tomato purée, a little at a time, continuing to stir and fry. Finally, add salt, cinnamon, cloves, cayenne pepper and 450 ml (3/4 pint) of water. Bring to the boil, cover, lower heat, and simmer gently for 10 minutes.

Cut the lemon into 4 or 5 slices, discarding the end pieces, and remove the seeds. Add lemon slices along with the chicken pieces, fried onions, sugar and freshly ground pepper to the sauce, stir, and bring to the boil. Cover, lower heat, and simmer gently for 20 to 25 minutes or until chicken is tender, turning the pieces every now and then. If chicken sticks to bottom of pot, add a little more water. You should end up with a very thick sauce.

To serve: Empty contents of pot into shallow serving bowl. Arrange the cooked lemon slices on top of the chicken pieces. Serve with any rice d ish or with pooris or chapatis. For vegetables you could serve Carrots and Peas with Ginger and Green Coriander or cauliflower or any other vegetable you like. Almost any kind of dal would also complement the dish.

Chicken with tomato sauce and butter

Serves 6

The original version of this dish is to be had at the Moti Mahal restaurant in Delhi. There, the Tandoori Chicken (page 83) is cut into small serving sections and put into a rich sauce of creamed tomatoes, butter and spices.

---

4 chicken legs
2 chicken breasts
2 medium-sized onions, peeled and coarsely chopped
5 cloves garlic, peeled and coarsely chopped
a piece of fresh ginger, about 5 cm (2 inches) long and 2.5 cm (1 inch) wide, peeled and coarsely chopped
1 stick of cinnamon, 6.5–7.5 cm (2½–3 inches), broken up

seeds from 6 cardamom pods
8 whole cloves
1 tsp whole black peppercorns
2 bay leaves, crumbled
1 hot dried red pepper (or more, as and if desired), crumbled
6 tbsp vegetable oil
8 medium-sized tomatoes (tinned or fresh), peeled and finely chopped
1 tsp salt
4 tbsp lightly salted butter

Remove skin from all chicken pieces. Divide legs into drumstick and thigh, and quarter the breasts. Pat dry and put aside.

In the container of an electric blender, combine the onions, garlic, ginger, cinnamon, cardamom seeds, cloves, peppercorns, bay leaves, red pepper and 3 tbsp water. Blend until you have a smooth paste.

Heat the oil in a 25–30 cm (10–12 inch) casserole-type pot over a high flame. When hot, put in the chicken pieces, 4 or 5 at a time, and brown them quickly (about a minute on each side). Remove with a slotted spoon. You will need to brown the chicken in several batches.

Turn heat to medium and pour in the paste from the blender. (Keep face averted.) Stir and fry the paste for 5 minutes, scraping the bottom of the pot well as you do so. Now add the chopped tomatoes, 150 ml (¼ pint) water and the salt. Bring to the boil and cover. Turn heat to very low and simmer gently for 30 minutes, stirring every 6 or 7 minutes.

Add the chicken pieces to the pot, as well as any juices that may have collected. Bring to the boil, cover, and simmer over low heat for 25 to 30 minutes. Stir gently every 5 or 6 minutes to avoid sticking and burning. Be careful not to break the chicken pieces as you stir. Lift cover, turn up heat and burn off most of the liquid.

Cut the butter into 4 pats. Take the chicken off the heat. Drop in the pats of butter and stir them in gently. Serve immediately.

To serve: Place contents of pot in a warm dish and serve with Rice with Black-eyed Peas or naan. You could, if you like, also serve Onions Pickled in Vinegar as they do at the Moti Mahal Restaurant in Delhi.

Marinated grilled chicken

Serves 4–6

This is a simple recipe in which the marinade, a mixture of onions, ginger, garlic, cumin, coriander, vinegar and oil is made in the electric blender. The chicken is marinated, then grilled. It could also be barbecued over charcoal.

1.4-1.6 kg (3-3½ lb) chicken, preferably legs, thighs and breasts, or a whole chicken, cut into serving pieces

Marinade
2 medium-sized onions, peeled and coarsely chopped
4 cloves garlic, peeled and coarsely chopped
a piece of fresh ginger, about 2.5 cm (1 inch) long and 2.5 cm (1 inch) wide, peeled and coarsely chopped

2-3 fresh hot green chillies, or ¼–½ tsp cayenne pepper (optional)
1 tsp whole cumin seeds
1 tbsp ground coriander
150 ml (¼ pint) wine vinegar
150 ml (¼ pint) olive or vegetable oil
2 tsp salt
⅛ tsp freshly ground pepper

Garnish
fresh green coriander, chopped

Combine all the ingredients for the marinade in the container of an electric blender. Blend at high speed until you have a smooth paste.

Pull off and discard the skin from chicken pieces. Prick chicken all over with a fork and place in a bowl. Pour marinade over chicken. Cover and refrigerate for 2 to 3 hours (24 hours would be best).

Fifty minutes before serving, heat your grill. Remove chicken pieces from bowl and, with as much marinade clinging to them as possible, place on baking sheet lined with aluminium foil. Grill for 15 minutes on each side or until chicken gets well browned. (Adjust distance from grill so it does not brown too fast.)

To serve: Place chicken on a warm platter and sprinkle green coriander over it. Serve with a rice dish, a green vegetable and a dal.

Grilled chicken strips

Serves 6–8

Chicken breasts are boned, cut into narrow strips, and then mixed with a paste consisting of oil, vinegar, onion, ginger, garlic and fennel seed, and the 'hot' (*garam*) spices: cardamom, cloves, cinnamon, black peppercorns, etc. The chicken sits in the marinade for 4 to 5 hours. It is then grilled and served. This dish is very easy to prepare, since most of the work is done by the electric blender. Its taste is heavenly, lightly but definitely spiced. It is very versatile – I have successfully served it as an hors d'oeuvre with toothpicks, at lunches with salad, at big dinners along with a meat dish, and at picnics, having made it the night before. It tastes as good cold as it does hot.

1.4 kg (3 lb) chicken breasts, boned and skinned (weight after boning and skinning)

Marinade
5 tbsp olive or vegetable oil
4 tbsp red wine vinegar
1 medium-sized onion, peeled and chopped
1 whole head of garlic (each clove peeled and chopped)
a piece of fresh ginger, about 2.5 cm (1 inch) cube, peeled and chopped

2 tbsp whole fennel seeds
2 tbsp ground cumin
2 tsp ground coriander
seeds from 8 cardamom pods
1 tsp ground cinnamon
8 whole cloves
20 black peppercorns
$1/2$–$3/4$ tsp cayenne pepper (use as desired; these measures are for a mildly hot dish)
2 tsp salt
1 tbsp tomato purée

Combine all ingredients needed for the marinade in the container of an electric blender. Blend at high speed until you have a smooth paste.

Wipe all the chicken pieces thoroughly dry. Divide breasts in 2 sections and then cut each section into strips that are 4 or 5 cm (1$1/2$ or 2 inches) long and about 1 cm ($1/2$ inch) wide.

In a bowl combine the chicken and the marinade ˜d mix well. I use my hands to rub the marinade into the chicken pieces. ˌr and refrigerate 4 to 5 hours.

Preheat the grill (45 minutes before serving if you are going to eat it hot). Line a baking tray with aluminium foil. Spread the chicken (most of the marinade will cling to it) thinly on the tray. (You will need to do two batches unless you have an extra large grill.)

When the grill is well heated, put in the tray with the chicken. Grill for 10 minutes, turn the pieces over, and grill another 10 minutes, or until the chicken is lightly browned. Remove chicken pieces with a spatula and place in warm serving dish. Cover and keep in warm place. Do the second batch the same way. (I usually put the second batch in to grill and serve the first batch. As soon as people are ready for seconds, the next batch is almost ready.) Remember, this chicken will *not* have a uniformly dark-brown colour; it should be dark only in spots.

To serve: Place on warm platter and serve with a rice dish, a lamb dish if you are entertaining, a yogurt dish, and at least one vegetable. Serve as an appetizer with toothpicks. Eat it cold at picnics, also with the aid of toothpicks.

Roast chicken stuffed with spiced rice

Serves 4

If you are tired of your usual chicken roast, try this one. With the expenditure of just a wee bit more time and energy, you can create a sensational dish – spicy without being hot, simple without being dull!

I use precooked (usually left-over!) rice for the stuffing. Adjust the salt for the stuffing according to the saltiness of the precooked rice.

---

1 roasting chicken, 1.8 kg (4 lb)
(at room temperature)

Marinade
2 tbsp olive oil (or vegetable oil
1 tbsp lemon juice
1/4 tsp salt
1/8 tsp freshly ground pepper
1/2 tsp ground cumin
1/4 tsp ground garam masala

Stuffing
1 medium-sized onion, peeled and
coarsely chopped

2 cloves garlic, peeled and coarsely chopped
a piece of fresh ginger, about
2.5 cm (1 inch) cube, peeled and coarsely chopped
3 tomatoes (tinned or fresh), peeled and chopped
1 tsp ground coriander
1 tsp ground cumin
4 tbsp vegetable oil
1/4 tsp whole black mustard seeds
1/4 tsp whole cumin seeds
2 teacups (well-packed) cooked rice
1/2 tsp salt (or as needed)

Mix all the ingredients for the marinade. Wipe chicken well with a cloth or paper towel so it is as dry as possible. Brush three-fourths of the marinade all over the chicken, inside and out. Let the chicken sit, unrefrigerated, for about 2 hours. Save rest of marinade.

Preheat oven to 230°C (450°F) mark 8.

Place the onions, garlic, ginger, tomatoes, coriander, and cumin in the container of an electric blender. Blend at high speed until you have a smooth paste.

Heat the 4 tbsp of oil in a 25–30 cm (10–12 inch) frying-pan over medium-high flame. When very hot, drop in the mustard and cumin seeds. When the mustard seeds begin to rise and pop (15 to 30 seconds), add the paste from the blender, keeping face averted, as the mixture will bubble rapidly and splatter. Stirring, fry the paste on medium-high heat until it is browned. The oil should separate from the paste (this will take about 10 minutes). You will need to stir more frequently as the moisture evaporates.

Add the cooked rice, and the salt as and if you need it. Turn heat to low and mix the browned paste with the rice. Loosely stuff the thicken with the rice and truss it. Place it in an oven-proof baking dish, breast up, and put it in the preheated oven.

Let the chicken brown for about 20 minutes, basting it with the remaining marinade mixture every 5 minutes. Turn down the heat to 180°C (350°F) mark 4. Cook another hour or until the leg moves easily when pushed up and down at its socket. Baste every 10 minutes with the juices that will come out of the chicken.

To serve: Lift chicken gently and put on a warm platter. Let it sit for 15 minutes so juices will not flow out when carved. Serve simply with a green salad or, if you like, with any green beans, peas or cauliflower dish. Sweet Tomato Chutney also tastes good with this roast.

Murgh mussallam (whole chicken with spices)

Serves 4

In this royal dish, a whole chicken is first marinated in a paste consisting of garlic, ginger, turmeric, hot green chillies, garam masala, yogurt and salt for about 2 hours. It is then browned and simmered with a second paste made up of fried onions and garlic, ginger, almonds, lemon juice and an array of spices like cardamom, cinnamon, nutmeg, mace, etc. Hard-boiled eggs are put into the sauce about 10 minutes before the chicken is done and then arranged around the chicken.

1 whole chicken, about 1.6 kg (3½ lb)
1 tsp loosely packed leaf saffron
4 hard-boiled eggs

Marinade
6 cloves of garlic, peeled and
    coarsely chopped
a piece of fresh ginger, about
    5 cm (2 inches) long and 2.5 cm
    (1 inch) wide, peeled and
    coarsely chopped
1½ tsp salt
½ tsp garam masala
½ tsp ground turmeric
4 tbsp plain yogurt
2 fresh hot green chillies, sliced,
    or ¼–½ tsp cayenne pepper
    (optional)

Cooking paste
8 tbsp vegetable oil
4 medium-sized onions, peeled and
    coarsely chopped

4 cloves garlic, peeled and coarsely
    chopped
a piece of fresh ginger, about
    2.5 cm (1 inch) long and 2.5 cm
    (1 inch) wide, peeled and
    coarsely chopped
1 tbsp blanched almonds, slivered
1 tbsp ground coriander
1 tsp ground cumin
seeds from 4 large black or 8 small
    green cardamom pods
¼ tsp ground cloves
½ tsp ground cinnamon
¼ tsp ground nutmeg
¼ tsp ground mace
1½ tsp salt
¼ tsp freshly ground black pepper
½ tsp cayenne pepper (optional)
3 tbsp lemon juice

Garnish
2 tbsp finely chopped fresh green
    coriander

First make your marinade.
Put the ingredients for the marinade into the electric blender. Blend at high speed until you have a smooth paste.

Peel the skin off the whole chicken. Where it is hard to peel, as on the wing tips, you can leave it on. Prick the chicken all over with a fork, place in a bowl, and pour marinade over it. Rub the chicken well with the marinade, both inside and out, and leave, unrefrigerated, about 2 hours.

Rinse out your blender container. You will need it again.

Soak the saffron in 2 tbsp of hot water.

Now make the paste to cook the chicken in. Heat 6 tbsp of the vegetable oil in a 25–30 cm (10–12 inch) heavy-bottomed pot over a medium-high flame. When hot, put in the chopped onions, garlic and ginger. Stir and fry for 8 to 10 minutes or until the onions are brown at the edges but still soft. With a slotted spoon, remove onions, garlic and ginger and place them in the blender container. Reserve the cooking oil.

Place a small iron or aluminium frying-pan over a medium flame. When it is hot, put the blanched almonds in it. Stir them around until they turn golden, then add them to the blender container. In the same small frying-pan put the ground coriander and cumin. Stir, watching, until the spices turn a few shades darker (do *not* let them burn). They will smoke quite a bit, but don't worry – it is to be expected. Then put them in the blender along with the cardamom seeds, cloves, cinnamon, nutmeg, mace, salt, black pepper, cayenne, lemon juice and 150 ml (1/4 pint) of water. Blend all to a smooth paste, pausing, if necessary, to push the mixture down with a rubber spatula a few times.

When the chicken has marinated for 2 hours, heat the reserved oil and add 2 more tbsp of oil to it. Do this over medium-high flame. Lift the chicken out of the bowl along with any clinging marinade and place in the oil. Brown it as well as you can on all sides. You will not be able to do this too evenly, but it does not matter.

When the chicken has browned, turn heat down to low. Take the paste from the blender and, using a rubber spatula, spread it all over the chicken. Add 300 ml (1/2 pint) of water to the pot and bring to the boil. Cover tightly. Turn heat to low and simmer gently for about 40 minutes or until chicken is tender. Turn chicken 2 or 3 times during the first 15 minutes of this cooking time. After that, leave it breast up and baste it every 5 to 7 minutes with the sauce.

Peel the hard-boiled eggs, and 10 minutes before the chicken is fully cooked put them in the pot, spooning some sauce over them as well. Pour saffron and saffron water over chicken. Cover and continue simmering until chicken is tender.

To serve: Lift chicken carefully out of pot and place it on warmed platter. Arrange eggs around it. If you like, skim the oil off the sauce before pouring it over chicken and eggs. Sprinkle with chopped green coriander. Serve with Rice with Peas. You could also serve any vegetable you like: Fried Aubergines with Sour Green Chutney, or a cauliflower or bean dish might be nice. A yogurt relish is almost a must with Murgh Mussallam. I often serve Yogurt with Spinach.

Duck – stuffed and roasted

Serves 2

The duck here is stuffed with rice, spices, raisins and nuts to make a superbly festive meal. I find that a 1.8–2 kg (4–4 1/2 lb) duck really serves only two people well. It has a large cavity inside and rather small legs. Most of the meat is around the breast area, and that is not too much.

1 duck, 1.8–2 kg (4–4½ lb), at room temperature – liver, gizzard and heart included
2 tbsp vegetable oil
½ tsp whole cumin seeds
½ tsp whole fennel seeds
15 fenugreek seeds
1 medium-sized onion, finely chopped
a piece of fresh ginger, 2.5 cm (1 inch) long and 1 cm (½ inch) wide, grated or minced
1 hot green chilli, cut into thin rounds, or ⅛–¼ tsp cayenne pepper (optional)

1 tbsp tomato purée mixed with 2 tbsp water
3 tbsp minced fresh green coriander
2 teacups cooked rice
2 tbsp golden raisins
1 tbsp dried apricots, chopped to the size of raisins
3 tbsp pine nuts or slivered blanched almonds
½ tsp salt (more if the rice is unsalted)
⅛ tsp freshly ground black pepper
1½ tsp lemon juice
1½ tsp sugar
additional salt, pepper

Prick the skin of the duck with a fork to allow the lining of fat to ooze out as it melts. Mince the liver, gizzard, and heart.

Preheat oven to 230°C (450°F) mark 8.

Heat the oil in a 25–30 cm (10–12 inch) frying-pan over medium-high flame, and add the cumin, fennel and fenugreek seeds. Stir. When the cumin seeds begin to darken (this will take 10 to 20 seconds) add the onions, ginger and green chilli if you wish to use it. Fry, stirring, for about 2 minutes or until onions turn a little brown. Now add at intervals, continuing to stir and fry, the minced liver, gizzard and heart; after a minute or two, the tomato purée and minced green coriander; in another 2 minutes, the cooked rice, turning heat to low; and finally, the raisins, apricots and pine nuts or almonds, mixing everything well. Stir and fry another 5 minutes.

Season with salt, cayenne pepper (if you wish to use it instead of the green chilli), black pepper, lemon juice and sugar.

Stuff the duck loosely with the mixture in the frying-pan, truss, place it in roasting pan breast up, and set in the preheated oven.

Let duck brown for 20 to 25 minutes. There is no need to baste. Remove fat with a bulb baster as it accumulates in roasting pan.

Turn heat to 180°C (350°F) mark 4, and let duck cook for another 1½ hours, or until the juices of the bird run a clear yellow when it is pricked.

To serve: Place duck on a warm serving platter. Sprinkle skin with a little salt and freshly ground pepper. Serve with green beans or peas, or with a simple green salad if you like.

Chicken Moghlai

Serves 6

This rich, elaborate, saffron-flavoured dish justifies the time taken in preparing it by its exquisite taste and appearance. It has a burnt-red colour and smells of cardamom, cloves and cinnamon. It tastes even better if you cook it a night before serving it, thus allowing the sauce to act as a marinade for the chicken.

I use legs, thighs and breasts of chicken for this recipe, but you could buy a whole 1.25–1.4 kg (2½–3 lb) chicken and have it cut into small-ish serving portions. It may, then, feed only 4 people. You could also use 6 whole quail, skinned, or 6 whole partridges, skinned.

1.25-1.4 kg (2½-3 lb) chicken legs, thighs and breasts
4 medium-sized onions, 2 peeled and chopped and 2 cut into half lengthwise, then sliced into thin half-rings
a piece of fresh ginger, about 4 cm (1½ inches) long and 2.5 cm (1 inch) wide, peeled and chopped
8 cloves garlic, peeled and chopped
10 tbsp vegetable oil
2 cinnamon sticks, 6.5–7.5 cm (2½– 3 inches) long
2 bay leaves
10 cardamom pods, slightly crushed

10 whole cloves
1 tsp whole cumin seed
1½ tbsp ground coriander ⎫
½ tbsp ground cumin ⎬ Dry-roasted together
⎭
½ tsp ground turmeric
¼–½ tsp cayenne pepper
3 tbsp yogurt
1 medium-sized tomato (tinned or fresh), peeled and finely chopped
1-1½ tsp salt
1 well-packed tsp leaf saffron, roasted and crumbled
1 tbsp warm milk

Skin the chicken pieces. Quarter the breasts and divide the legs into drumstick and thigh. Pat chicken dry and set aside.

Put the chopped onions, ginger and garlic in the container of an electric blender along with 4 tbsp of water. Blend at high speed until you have a smooth paste.

In a 25 cm (10 inch) heavy-bottomed pot, heat 7 tbsp of the oil. Put in the sliced onions and fry, stirring, over a medium-high flame for 10 to 12 minutes or until onions are dark brown and crisp but not black and burned. Remove them with a slotted spoon and set aside in bowl or plate.

Raise heat to high and put the chicken pieces in the same oil a few at a time. Without letting chicken cook too much, brown to as dark a colour as possible. Remove each batch to a platter.

Tandoori chicken – my version

Serves 6–8

There are two things that I need to point out here. The chickens used for the *tandoor* in India are usually spring chickens, weighing 900 g – 1.25 kg (2–2½ lb) each. They are cooked whole, with only wings and neck removed, on all sides at once. I find it more convenient to marinate and cook the chicken cut in pieces (it is also easier to serve and to eat this way). I buy the legs and breasts of grilling or frying chickens.

The chicken in this recipe should be marinated for about 24 hours. Assuming that most people like both dark and light meat, I am allocating one whole leg and half a breast for each of 6 people.

1 medium-sized onion, peeled and coarsely chopped
6 whole cloves garlic, peeled and coarsely chopped
a piece of fresh ginger, about 5 cm (2 inches) long and 2.5 cm (1 inch) wide, peeled and coarsely chopped
3 tbsp lemon juice
225 g (8 oz) plain yogurt
1 tbsp ground coriander
1 tsp ground cumin
1 tsp ground turmeric
1 tsp garam masala
¼ tsp ground mace
¼ tsp ground nutmeg
¼ tsp ground cloves
¼ tsp ground cinnamon

4 tbsp olive oil (or vegetable oil)
2 tsp salt
¼ tsp freshly ground black pepper
¼–½ tsp cayenne pepper (optional, or use as desired)
½–1 tsp orange food colouring (use the Spanish bijol, or Indian powdered food colouring, or Bush's orange-red powder; its use is optional)
6 chicken legs
3 chicken breasts, halved

Garnish
1 medium-sized onion
2 lemons
extra lemon juice (optional)

Make the marinade first. Put the chopped onions, garlic, ginger and lemon juice in an electric blender, and blend to a smooth paste, about 1 minute at high speed. Place this in a bowl large enough to accommodate the chicken. Add the yogurt, coriander, cumin, turmeric, garam masala, mace, nutmeg, cloves, cinnamon, olive oil, salt, black pepper, cayenne and food colouring. Mix thoroughly.

Skin the chicken legs and breasts. With a sharp knife make 3 diagonal slashes on each breast section, going halfway down to the bone. Make 2 diagonal slashes on each thigh, also going halfway down to the bone. With the point of a sharp knife, make 4 or 5 jabs on each drumstick.

Put the chicken in the marinade and rub the marinade into the slashes with your finger. Cover and leave refrigerated for 24 hours. Turn 4 or 5 times while the chicken is marinating.

About 1½ hours before serving, light your charcoal. It should take 20 to 30 minutes to get red hot. Place the grill on its lowest notch.

Peel the onion for garnishing and slice it paper-thin. Separate the rings and set in a small bowl of ice water, cover, and refrigerate.

When the fire is hot, lift out the chicken pieces and place on the grill. Cook about 7 or 8 minutes on each side, then raise the grill a few notches to cook more slowly for another 15 to 20 minutes on each side. Baste with marinade as you cook.

To serve: Warm a large platter. Place the chicken pieces on it. Drain the water from the onion rings and lay them on top of the chicken. Quarter the lemons lengthwise and place them around the chicken. The chicken tastes very good with extra lemon juice squeezed on it.

This chicken is considered a delicacy and can be served at a banquet with Pullao, naans, a few vegetable dishes, and onions pickled in vinegar.

Try it also with Rice with Spinach.

Chicken biryani

Serves 6–8

Biryani is perhaps one of our most elaborate rice dishes. Of Moghul origin, it is cooked with lamb or chicken, streaked with saffron, and garnished with raisins and nuts. The chicken is first marinated for at least 2 hours in a delicious paste of ginger, garlic, onions, yogurt, lemon juice and spices. It is then cooked briefly. Partially cooked rice is placed over it, and the chicken and rice are allowed to steam for about an hour.

6 medium-sized onions
4 cloves garlic, peeled and coarsely
  chopped
a piece of fresh ginger, about 5 cm
  (2 inches) long and 2.5 cm
  (1 Inch) wlde, peeled and
  coarsely chopped
10 whole cloves
20 whole black peppercorns
seeds from 8 whole cardamom
  pods
2 tsp leaf saffron, loosely packed,
  roasted and crumbled
1/4 tsp ground mace
41/2 tsp salt
3 tbsp lemon juice
285 g (10 oz) plain yogurt
8 tbsp vegetable oil

2 bay leaves
4 large black cardamoms, if
  available
900 g (2 lb) chicken legs and
  breasts
1/4 tsp ground clnnamon
1 tsp ground coriander
1 tsp ground cumin
1 tsp whole poppy seeds
2 tbsp milk
340 g (12 oz) long-grain rice

Garnishes
2 tbsp golden raisins, fried
2 tbsp blanched almonds
2 hard-boiled eggs, sliced or
  quartered lengthwise

First you have to make the marinade for the chicken.
Peel and coarsely chop 3 of the onions.

Place chopped onion, garlic and ginger in an electric blender, along with the cloves, peppercorns, the seeds only from the 8 cardamoms, cinnamon, coriander, cumin, poppy seeds, mace, 1½ tsp salt and the lemon juice. Blend all of these at high speed until you have a smooth paste. Place this paste in a large bowl. Add the yogurt and mix well.

Now peel the 3 remaining onions. Slice them into very fine rings, and halve all the rings.

In a 25 cm (10 inch) heavy-bottomed frying-pan, heat the oil over medium flame. When hot, add the bay leaves and 4 black cardamoms. Fry for about 10 to 15 seconds. Now put in the onions and fry them, stirring, for about 10 minutes or until they get brown and crisp (but *not* burned). Remove them carefully with a slotted spoon, squeezing out as much of the oil as possible. Reserve all the onion-flavoured oil, the black cardamoms and the bay leaves. You will need them later. Mix in two-thirds of the fried onions with the marinade paste. Place the rest on a paper towel to drain. Set aside for garnishing.

Remove skin from the chicken legs and breasts. Cut the legs into two pieces each (drumstick and thigh), and quarter all the breasts. Pierce the chicken pieces with a fork and place in the bowl with the marinade paste. Mix well. Cover the bowl and refrigerate for at least 2 hours. Turn occasionally.

After 2 hours (or more), remove the bowl from the refrigerator and place all its contents in a 3.4–4.5 litre (6-8 pint) heavy-bottomed pot. Bring slowly to the boil, cover, lower heat, and simmer for 15 minutes. Remove only the chicken pieces, place them in a 5.7 litre (10 pint) casserole dish, and cover. Set aside. On a medium flame, boil down the marinade paste, stirring, until you have about 9 to 10 tbsp left. Spoon the paste over the chicken. Cover again.

Preheat oven to 150°C (300°F) mark 2.

Soak the saffron in 2 tbsp hot (not boiling) milk.

Bring about 2.8 litres (5 pints) of water with 3 tbsp of salt to the boil in a 3.4 litre (6 pint) pot, then add the rice. After it has come to the boil again, cook 5 minutes, timing very carefully (the rice must not cook through). Drain the rice in a colander, then place it on top of the chicken in the casserole. Pour the saffron milk over the rice, streaking it with orange lines. Spoon out the onion-flavoured oil from the pan, reserving a level tablespoon to fry the raisins if you like. Sprinkle the oil, cardamom and bay leaves over the rice. Cover the casserole dish with aluminium foil, cut 5 cm (2 inches) wider than the rim of the dish. Now put the lid on and use the protruding foil edges to seal the dish as best you can by crinkling it and pushing it against the sides. Bake 1 hour.

Garnishes: There are several garnishes that can be used for *biryani*; you can use them all, or only what you like, but the fried onions are a must. If you wish to use raisins, you can fry them in a tablespoon of the onion-flavoured oil just after you have fried the onions.

To serve: As you lift the cover off your casserole dish, you will see beautiful saffron streaks on the white rice. Spoon the rice and chicken out onto a large platter. Sprinkle fried onions and other garnishes of your choice over, and serve hot. With Biryani, serve Koftas and some yogurt dish – Yogurt with Potatoes. If you wish to serve a vegetable, Cauliflower with Ginger and Green Coriander would be very good.

Biryani is quite definitely not an everyday dish. It is served at weddings and important dinners. Try serving it at a late supper party. It was, and is, a dish worthy of a king.

VEGETABLES

Indian vegetable markets are an absolute delight to the eye and a source of great anticipatory glee to the palate. India produces most of the kinds of fruit and vegetables found in Britain and many, many more. But, of course, everything is seasonal. You can expect corn only in August, September and October, mangoes only in the summer, cauliflower only in the winter, and fresh mushrooms only during the humid monsoons. So a change of seasons for us is more than just a change of weather. Our menu changes considerably, and for most Indians who are vegetarians it changes drastically. If you eat carrot 'water pickles' in the winter, you eat watermelon-rind pickles in the summer, and if you eat tangerines, guavas and apples in the winter, you can have melons, loquats and *cheekoos* (a kind of round, all-brown persimmon) in the summer. There are no frozen vegetables or fruit to be had all year round, and no large-scale hot-houses raising out-of-season vegetables. India does, now, produce varieties of dried vegetables, but they are used rather rarely. Winter is our good vegetable season, and summer brings the most luscious varieties of fruit.

When an Indian housewife goes shopping and buys about 50 pence worth of vegetables, the shopkeeper, if he is friendly, will throw in a handful of green chillies and a bunch of fresh green coriander free. These two items are, as you may have already noted in many recipes, essential to a lot of our cooking. The Indian housewife will also stock up on ginger, considering herself very lucky indeed if she manages to find the young, tender ginger. This has many advantages. Its skin can be lightly scraped instead of peeled; the tough fibres have not yet developed so it can be used for an instant relish which combines ginger slices, lime juice and salt; it can also be cut, chopped, grated, or minced with much greater ease. This young ginger looks slightly pink, and if you ever happen to see it in some store, do buy it.

Onions are another important vegetable. Raw, they are used for relishes and garnishing. Ground, they are used to make the paste in which some vegetables and meats are cooked. They can be sautéed or fried and then cooked along with cauliflower or aubergine or used as stuffing for okra pods.

India grows many varieties of mushrooms, the most delicious (and expensive) of which is one that grows in Kashmir and resembles a heart-shaped black sponge! Since I have been unable to find the small, slim mushroom commonly seen in North India, my recipes are adapted to the commercial variety found in most English grocery stores.

Indians eat a lot of greens – fenugreek greens, mustard greens, white radish greens, gram (or chickpea) greens and, of course, spinach. Each is seasonal, and each area has traditional ways of cooking its greens. In northern India, where I come from, fenugreek greens, being very strong-flavoured, are nearly always cooked with tiny new potatoes in their jackets, or with carrots. The Punjab, in north-western India, is famous for its creamed mustard greens, which both the poorest and the richest Punjabi serves with flat corn bread and a glass of buttermilk. A very popular dish in Bengal is *chorchuri* in which various greens are first sautéed and then allowed to simmer gently with fried fish-heads. When cooking white radishes, we tend to use both the radish and its leaves. Chickpea, or gram, greens, which I used to eat raw with salt and pepper, are not to be found in this country. Spinach, which is popular throughout India, is often creamed, or dipped in batter and fried, or cooked with meat.

Corn, in India, is available only during the late summer months. The fresh cobs, peeled and roasted, are sold on street corners, rather like chestnuts. The corn seller carries a light, portable charcoal stove on which he roasts his corn, and he sells it sprinkled with salt, red pepper, black pepper and lime juice. I have tried roasting the hybrid 'sweet corn' available in most English shops, but it is too tender, and very often it just shrivels up. The only times I have been successful have been with what the English would call the 'tougher' ears of corn. If you ever do manage to find some 'tougher' ears which won't 'melt in your mouth', peel them and roast them over charcoal. They can be superb. And don't, for heaven's

sake, put butter on them. Eat them either plain or sprinkled with salt, freshly ground pepper, and a little lime or lemon juice.

Potatoes are a popular staple throughout North India. Not only are they
cooked in combination with meats, other vegetables, rice and dals, but
they are also cooked with every imaginable permutation of spices. A young
child may want his potatoes boiled and then fried with cumin seeds; at a
picnic one might have 'dry' potatoes cooked with red peppers, fenugreek,
fennel, cumin and mustard seeds; at a banquet one might be served
potatoes cooked with yogurt and the *garam masalas*, cinnamon, cloves,
cardamom, bay leaves, etc; and of course, there is my favourite, Potatoes
cooked with Asafetida and Cumin, a 'wet' dish best enjoyed with pooris.

A vegetable that was once basically ignored in Britain, is the aubergine.
Still, it seems confined to the occasional parmigiana, moussaka, or
ratatouille. It deserves better. Stuffed, baked and roasted pulp, when
mixed with yogurt and fresh mint, makes a refreshing summer 'salad'.
Deep-fried in slices and smothered in one of many sour chutneys, it can
serve as an appetizer or an accompanying vegetable dish.

I can't really begin to list all the Indian vegetables and fruit. We have a
'pickling' carrot that is dark red, like a beetroot; during late winter, Indians
buy green chickpeas, or *chholas*, which can be cooked or eaten raw; our
sweet potato has the consistency of a crumbly baking potato; we eat lotus
stems and water chestnuts; we have *jamuns* and *falsas* and *bair* and
kaseru and *parval* – fruits and vegetables which don't even have any
English names. And this list could go on and on.

The recipes in this chapter are mostly for vegetables that can be found
in supermarkets – beans, carrots, cauliflower, cabbage, aubergines, peas,
potatoes, etc. I do have some recipes for okra which should be cooked
only when fresh pods are available.

Fried aubergines with sour green chutney

Serves 6

---

1 packed teacup chopped fresh
  green coriander
1 fresh hot green chilli, washed and
  finely sliced, or 1/4 tsp cayenne
  pepper (optional)
225 g (8 oz) plain yogurt
1/2 tsp salt (a little more if you need
  it; sometimes yogurt is more
  sour than at other times)
1/2 tsp roasted, ground cumin seeds
1 tbsp lemon juice
vegetable oil for deep frying

6 small, oval aubergines or 1 large
  one (aubergines come in so
  many sizes that after reading this
  recipe, I'm afraid you have to be
  your own judge about how many
  you need)
8 fenugreek seeds
1/2 tsp fennel seeds
1/2 tsp black onion seeds (kalonji), if
  available
1/4 tsp cumin seeds
salt
freshly ground black pepper

For the chutney: Put green coriander and chilli in blender with 3 tbsp water and blend until smooth paste (about 1 minute). You may need to push coriander down a couple of times.

In a bowl, combine yogurt, salt, roasted ground cumin seeds, lemon juice and the paste from blender. Cover and refrigerate chutney until ready for use.

Ten minutes before eating time, heat oil at a depth of 4–5 cm (1 1/2– 2 inches) in frying-pan, wok or *karhai* over medium heat. While heating, wash and dry aubergines. If you have the small, oval ones, quarter them lengthwise, preserving the stem and the sepals. If you have a very large one, quarter it lengthwise and slice each quarter into 1 cm (1/2 inch) thick pieces.

When oil is very hot, add the fenugreek, fennel, onion and cumin seeds. After 10 or 20 seconds, drop in as many aubergine pieces as the container will hold in one layer. Deep-fry each batch until golden-brown. Drain on paper towels, sprinkle each batch with salt and freshly ground pepper, and place in a warm dish. When the aubergines have fried, spoon one-quarter of the cold chutney over them and serve immediately. Serve the rest of the chutney on the side.

To serve: While the aubergine fries, I usually put all the rest of my dinner into serving dishes and bring them to the table. I bring the aubergine dish out last. This dish is usually served at meals along with other vegetables. It is very rarely the only vegetable at the table. Try it as a Sunday lunch along with Prawns with Dill and Ginger, Rice with Black-eyed Peas, and green beans.

You can also cut the aubergine fairly small, insert toothpicks and serve it with drinks.

Aubergine bharta (smoked aubergine)

Serves 4–6

Until the advent of gas, most cooking in India was done on wood or coal, and one of the waste products of wood and coal is, of course, ash. Not wishing to waste even a waste product, we geared our cuisine so that while some foods were cooking on top of the flame, others were being roasted in the ashes.

One vegetable that was roasted was the aubergine. Once roasted, it was peeled and the inside was either mixed with chopped raw onion, fresh mint and yogurt or cooked further with onions and tomatoes – which is the recipe I'm going to give you now.

Lacking ashes in my 'modern' kitchen, I roast the aubergine right on top of the stove over an open flame. This is a bit messy, so I would advise you to insert an aluminium burner liner before you start.

1 large aubergine, preferably with a stem	½ fresh hot green chilli, finely sliced (optional)
1 medium-sized onion, peeled and coarsely chopped	1 tbsp chopped fresh green coriander; reserve a little for garnishing
a piece of fresh ginger, about 2.5 cm (1 inch) square, peeled and coarsely chopped	2 medium-sized tomatoes (tinned or fresh), peeled and coarsely chopped
2 cloves garlic, peeled and coarsely chopped	¾-1 tsp salt (according to size of aubergine)
5 tbsp vegetable oil	1 tsp lemon juice
½ tsp ground turmeric	1 tsp garam masala

Line your gas burner with aluminium foil. (If you have an electric stove, place the aubergine under a preheated grill, and turn it around until it is blackened on all sides, although it will never taste quite as smoky as when done over a flame.) Stand your aubergine, stalk up, directly over a medium-low flame. Leave it there until the bottom has burned black and looks completely scorched. Now lay it on its side. As soon as the area nearest the flame darkens and turns soft, turn the aubergine slightly. Use the stem of the aubergine to turn with. Keep turning until the whole aubergine is done. (You could use tongs, but take care not to burst the aubergine or you will have a big mess.) As more and more of the aubergine is 'scorched' it will turn softer and be more difficult to handle. Don't give up. This whole process will take 20 to 25 minutes.

Once the aubergine is 'smoked', put it on a plate and carry it to the sink. Put it under cold running water and peel the blackened outer skin under the running water. Drain, shaking off as much water as you can.

Put the peeled inside of the aubergine on a chopping board and chop it coarsely. Set aside in a plate or bowl.

Put the onion, ginger and garlic in a blender with 3 tbsp of water and blend to a paste at high speed.

Heat the oil in a frying-pan over medium heat. While heating, pour in the paste from the blender and add the turmeric. Fry this mixture, stirring frequently; after about 5 minutes, when it begins to turn brown, add the green chilli and the green coriander; then after about 1 minute, the chopped tomatoes. Lower the flame and cook for 10 minutes, stirring occasionally. Finally, add the chopped aubergine, raise the flame to medium low, and fry, stirring, for 10 to 15 minutes, seasoning with the salt, lemon juice and garam masala.

To serve: Remove the bharta to a warm dish and serve sprinkled with green coriander. It is best when eaten with pooris or hot chapatis. Serve Khare Masale Ka Gosht with it.

Sweet-and-sour aubergine

Serves 6

Though normally served hot, this aubergine dish may also be served cold at a buffet or picnic.

900 g (2 lb) aubergine	2 tsp ground amchoor or lemon juice
2 tsp salt	2¹/₂ tsp sugar
1 medium-sized onion	¹/₈–¹/₄ tsp cayenne pepper
vegetable oil for shallow frying	1 tbsp roasted and lightly crushed
1 tbsp panchphoran	sesame seeds

Cut off the stem ends of the aubergines and quarter them lengthwise. Cut the quarters crosswise into 1 cm (¹/₂ inch) thick slices and put in a sieve set over a bowl. Sprinkle with the salt and mix well. Set aside for 30 to 45 minutes. Pat dry.

Peel the onion, slice it in half, then cut into 0.5 cm (¹/₄ inch) slices.

Heat 1 cm (¹/₂ inch) oil in a 22 cm (9 inch) wide frying-pan over a medium-high flame. When hot, put in as many slices of the aubergine as the pan will hold in a single layer. Fry for about 3 minutes on each side or until aubergine slices turn a medium reddish-brown colour. Remove with a slotted spatula and set aside. Do all the aubergine this way.

Pour off all but 3 tbsp of the oil in the frying-pan and turn heat to medium. Put in the panchphoran. Within a second or two, the spices will begin to sizzle and pop. As soon as that happens, put in the sliced onion. Stir and fry until the onion just starts to turn brown at the edges. Now put in the fried aubergine, amchoor, sugar, cayenne, and sesame seeds. Stir gently and cook for 1 minute.

Aubergine cooked with crushed mustard seeds and yogurt

Serves 4

This quick-cooking dish from eastern India uses three ingredients that are very typical of Bengali cooking – mustard oil, panchphoran and crushed black mustard seeds.

450-675 g (1–1¹/₂ lb) aubergine	1¹/₂ tsp salt
1¹/₂ tbsp whole black mustard seeds	250 ml (8 fl oz) yogurt
¹/₈ tsp cayenne pepper	¹/₈ tsp freshly ground black pepper
7 tbsp mustard oil or vegetable oil	¹/₄ tsp freshly ground cardamom
1 tbsp panchphoran	seeds

Discard the stem end of the aubergine and dice aubergine into 2.5 cm (1 inch) cubes.

Grind the mustard seeds lightly in a coffee grinder and then empty into a bowl. Add the cayenne and 250 ml (8 fl oz) water. Mix and set aside. Heat the oil in a 30 cm (12 inch) frying or sauté pan over a medium-high flame. When hot, put in the panchphoran. Stir the spices once. Immediately put in the mustard seed mixture, the cubed aubergine and 1 tsp salt. Keep stirring and cooking over a medium-high flame until most of the liquid is absorbed. Add another 250 ml (8 fl oz) of water, cover, and turn heat to low. Simmer gently for about 15 minutes or until aubergine pieces are quite tender. Remove cover and turn up heat to boil off about half the liquid.

Just before serving, beat the yogurt and 1/2 tsp salt with a fork until it becomes a smooth paste and pour the yogurt over the aubergine. Heat through but do not bring to the boil. Sprinkle black pepper and ground cardamom over the aubergine, stir, and serve at once.

Green beans with ginger

Serves 4–6

This dish is simple to make and has a very fresh, gingery taste.

675 g (1 1/2 lb) fresh green beans	3 tbsp chopped fresh green
a piece of fresh ginger, about 5 cm	coriander
(2 inches) long and 2.5 cm	1 tsp ground cumin
(1 inch) wide, peeled and	2 tsp ground coriander
coarsely chopped	1 1/4 tsp garam masala
6 tbsp vegetable oil	2 tsp lemon juice (or to taste)
1/4 tsp ground turmeric	1 tsp salt (or to taste)
1/2 fresh hot green chilli (optional),	
washed and sliced very finely	

Wash the green beans and trim the ends. Slice into fine rounds, 3-5 mm (1/8-1/4 inch) thick. When all the beans are chopped, set aside in a bowl.

Put the ginger in the blender with 3 tbsp of water and blend at high speed until it is a smooth paste.

Heat the oil in a 25 cm (10 inch) frying-pan over medium heat. While it is heating, pour in paste from blender and add turmeric. Fry, stirring constantly, for 2 minutes, then add the sliced green chillies and the green coriander, and after another minute, put in the green beans and continue cooking and stirring for about a minute. Add the cumin, coriander, 1 tsp of the garam masala, lemon juice, salt and 3 tbsp of warm water. Cover frying-pan, turn flame very low, and let beans cook slowly for about 40 minutes, stirring every 10 minutes or so.

To serve: These beans can easily be cooked in advance and reheated. Serve them in a warm dish, with 1/4 tsp garam masala sprinkled on top.

They go well with nearly all meat and chicken dishes. They can be eaten with plain boiled rice and Moong Dal, or served with hot pooris or parathas or chapatis.

Green beans with fresh coconut and sesame seeds

Serves 4

---

60 g (2 oz) freshly grated coconut (about 8 tbsp)
4 tbsp finely chopped fresh green coriander, or parsley
A generous pinch of crushed asafetida (optional)
1/2-1 fresh hot green chilli, finely chopped

1/2 tsp plus 1 tbsp salt
450 g (1 lb) fresh green beans, trimmed and cut into 2.5 cm (1 inch) lengths
6 tbsp ghee or vegetable oil
2 tbsp sesame seeds
1 tbsp whole black mustard seeds
1/8-1/4 tsp cayenne pepper (optional)

Combine the coconut, fresh coriander, asafetida, green chilli and 1/4 tsp salt in a bowl. Rub mixture well with your hands. Set aside.

Add 1 tbsp salt to 2 litres (3 1/2 pints) of water and bring to the boil in a large pot. Add the cut beans. Boil rapidly for 3 to 4 minutes or until beans are tender but still bright green and crisp. Drain in a colander and refresh by moving the colander under cold running water. Set aside.

Heat ghee or oil in a 25–30 cm (10–12 inch) wide sauté pan or heavy pot over a medium flame. When hot, put in the sesame and mustard seeds. As soon as the mustard seeds begin to pop, add the cayenne pepper. Stir once and add the beans. Sauté the beans over medium-low heat for 1 to 2 minutes or until they are heated through and well coated with the seeds. Add 1/4 tsp salt and stir. Now add the coconut-coriander mixture, stir once, and remove from heat. Serve immediately.

Cabbage with onions

Serves 4–6

I find that one medium-sized head of cabbage will feed 4 people easily. It can be stretched to 6 if there are many other dishes. As with most of our vegetables, we tend to overcook cabbage, but the end result tastes very good, so who cares!

---

1 medium-sized head of cabbage
2½ medium-sized onions
9 tbsp vegetable oil
6 whole fenugreek seeds
½ tsp whole cumin seeds
½ tsp whole black mustard seeds
½ tsp whole fennel seeds
2 cloves garlic, peeled and coarsely chopped

a piece of fresh ginger, 2.5 x 4 cm (1 x 1½ inches) peeled and coarsely chopped
1 medium-sized tomato (tinned or fresh), peeled
½ tsp ground turmeric
½–1 hot green chilli, thinly sliced (optional)
³/₄–1 tsp salt
1 tsp garam masala
1 tbsp lemon juice

Trim away the outer damaged leaves of the cabbage, wash it, and cut it in quarters. Remove the stem and hard core and shred cabbage lengthwise as finely as you can.

Peel 2 of the onions and cut them each into half, lengthwise. Now slice finely into half-circles.

Heat 6 tbsp of the oil in a 25 cm (10 inch) heavy-bottomed pot over medium heat, and add the fenugreek, cumin, mustard and fennel seeds. As the seeds start sizzling and changing colour (about 10 seconds), put in the sliced onions. Fry them over medium heat for about 3 minutes. Add the shredded cabbage, stir a few times, put the lid on, lower flame, and cook for 15 minutes.

Uncover and cook over fairly low heat for 30 minutes, stirring occasionally to prevent burning.

Meanwhile, peel and coarsely chop the remaining ½ onion and put it with the garlic, ginger and peeled tomato in electric blender. Blend to a paste.

In a frying-pan heat the 3 remaining tbsp of oil. Add the paste from the blender, the turmeric and the green chilli. Fry, stirring all the time, for 8 to 10 minutes (adding, if necessary, 1 tsp of warm water at a time to prevent sticking). When the cabbage has cooked for 30 minutes, add this fried paste mixture, along with the salt, garam masala and lemon juice. Stir and let it cook for another 5 minutes.

To serve: Serve with parathas, pooris, or chapatis. If serving with rice, serve karhi or dal and a chicken or meat dish like Chicken Cooked with Yogurt. Plain yogurt or Yogurt with Spinach would also go well with it.

Cabbage leaves stuffed with potatoes

Serves 6–8
Cabbage leaves can be stuffed with meat or potatoes. Here is my mother's recipe for the latter.

5 medium-sized potatoes	1 tsp garam masala
7 medium-sized onions	3½ tsp salt
10 tbsp vegetable oil	¼ tsp cayenne pepper (optional)
2 tsp whole fennel seeds	1 tbsp lemon juice
1 tsp whole cumin seeds	1 medium-sized head of cabbage

The stuffing: Boil the potatoes, then peel and dice them into 0.5 cm (¼ inch) pieces.

Peel the onions, cut them in half lengthwise, and slice them into fine half-circles.

In a frying-pan, heat 6 tbsp of the oil over medium heat. Add the onions, frying, stirring and separating the rings until the onions are brownish, for about 7 or 8 minutes; they should not get crisp.

Add the fennel and cumin seeds and fry for another 7 or 8 minutes on lower flame. The onions should look a rich reddish-brown now.

Add the diced boiled potatoes to the onion mixture and continue frying. As you fry, mash the potatoes with the back of a slotted spoon or potato masher.

To the potato and onion mixture add the *garam masala*, 2½ tsp salt, cayenne pepper if desired and lemon juice. Mix it all up and set aside, uncovered, to cool slightly.

The cabbage: Cut off the hard stem of the cabbage, remove the hard, damaged outer leaves, and wash it. In a pot large enough to hold the whole cabbage, bring to the boil water to which 1 tsp salt has been added. Drop the cabbage in (the water should cover at least three-quarters of it), cover, and allow to boil for 5 minutes. Lift cabbage out of boiling water, run under cold water, and carefully remove each leaf, taking care not to break it. Dry. If the inner leaves are still crisp, drop them again in the boiling water until they go limp. Remove and cool under cold water.

Spread out one leaf at a time. Snip out the hard core of the outer leaves with a sharp knife or a pair of kitchen shears. You can snip to about 2.5 cm (1 inch) into the leaf, removing a kind of narrow V. Now place a tablespoon of the stuffing in the centre of the leaf and fold the edges over. Put the stuffed leaf on your left palm and with your right palm gently squeeze out any extra moisture. This also helps to keep the stuffed cabbage leaves tightly closed.

In a 25 cm (10 inch) frying-pan, heat the remaining 4 tbsp of oil over medium-heat. Squeeze each stuffed cabbage leaf again between paper towels and put in frying-pan. Fry, a few pieces at a time, until each piece is browned on all sides. Take care not to let the leaves open. Remove them to a plate. When all the pieces are done, lower the heat, arrange the stuffed cabbage pieces in the frying-pan in tight layers, add 2 tablespoons water, cover, and cook on very low flame for 10 to 15 minutes.

To serve: Remove very carefully and serve on large, warm platter. Serve with Cubed Lamb with Onions and Raisins and Rice with Peas or with karhi, koftas, and plain boiled rice. This dish is also very good served with hot parathas.

Cabbage with yogurt

Serves 4

Here, as in many South Indian foods, a dried split pea – *urad dal* – is used as a seasoning. The dish is served warm, although I like it cold as well.

---

800 g (1³/₄ lb) green cabbage (¹/₂ medium-sized head)	1 medium-sized onion, peeled, cut in half lengthwise, then into 0.5 cm (¹/₄ inch) half rings
50 ml (2 fl oz) vegetable oil	
3 tbsp whole black mustard seeds	1¹/₂ tsp salt
2 tsp urad dal, picked over	45-60 g (1¹/₂–2 oz) cup freshly grated coconut
¹/₈–¹/₄ tsp cayenne pepper	
2 tsp ground coriander	250 ml (8 fl oz) plain yogurt

Remove the coarse outer leaves of the cabbage as well as its hard core. Now cut the cabbage evenly into 3 mm (1/8 inch) wide strips.

Heat the oil in a wok or a large sauté pan over a medium flame. When hot, put in the mustard seeds and urad dal. As soon as the mustard seeds begin to pop – this just takes a few seconds – put in the cayenne and the coriander. Stir once and quickly put in the cabbage and onion. Stir for 1 minute. Add the salt. Stir to mix. Cover, lower heat and cook about 5 to 8 minutes or until cabbage is just tender. Add the coconut and mix. Keep warm.

Put the yogurt in the top of a double boiler and beat until creamy. Heat. Stir continuously in one direction as it warms through. Do not let it get hot.

Put the cabbage into a warmed serving bowl. Then add the yogurt and fold it in.

Carrots and peas with ginger and green coriander

Serves 4–6

---

a piece of fresh ginger, 5 x 2.5 cm (2 x 1 inch), peeled and coarsely chopped
675 g (1 1/2 lb) young, slim carrots
6 tbsp vegetable oil
1/4 tsp whole black mustard seeds
5 whole fenugreek seeds
1/4 tsp ground turmeric
1 packed teacup coarsely chopped fresh green coriander

1 fresh hot green chilli, washed and finely sliced (optional, or substitute 1/4 tsp cayenne pepper)
450 g (1 lb) fresh peas, shelled
1 tsp ground coriander
1 tsp ground cumin
1 tsp garam masala
1 tsp salt

Put the ginger in blender with 3 tbsp of water and blend until smooth (about 1 minute).

Peel the carrots and slice them into rounds about 3 mm (1/8 inch) thick.

Heat the oil in a 25–30 cm (10–12 inch) frying-pan over medium heat. When very hot, add the mustard and fenugreek seeds. When mustard seeds begin to pop (10 to 20 seconds), put in the ginger paste and turmeric, keeping your face averted. Fry for about 2 minutes, stirring frequently. Add chopped green coriander and green chilli or cayenne, and cook, stirring, for another 2 minutes. Add carrots and peas and cook for 5 minutes more, stirring frequently.

Now put in the coriander, cumin, garam masala, salt and 3 tbsp of warm water. Stir for a minute, cover, lower heat, and cook slowly 30 minutes. Stir gently every 10 minutes or so.

To serve: Lift gently out of frying-pan and place on serving dish. Serve with hot pooris or parathas. This dish goes well with any sauced meat dish – Lamb with Onions and Mushrooms, etc. It is also good with Prawns with Dill and Ginger, plain Moong Dal, and Rice with Potatoes and Cumin Seed.

Cauliflower with ginger and green coriander

Serves 6–8

a piece of fresh ginger, about 6.5 x 2.5 cm (2½ x 1 inch), peeled and coarsely chopped
1 large head fresh cauliflower, or 2 small ones
8 tbsp vegetable oil
½ tsp ground turmeric
1 fresh hot green chilli, finely sliced, or ¼ tsp cayenne pepper (optional)

1 packed teacup coarsely chopped fresh green coriander
1 tsp ground cumin
2 tsp ground coriander
1 tsp garam masala
1 tbsp lemon juice
2 tsp salt

Put the ginger into a blender with 4 tbsp of water, and blend until it becomes smooth (about 1 minute).

Cut off the thick, coarse stem of the cauliflower and remove all leaves. First break the cauliflower into large flowerets, using your hands if it is a loosely packed head and a sharp knife if it is too tightly packed. Since you want to end up with small flowerets, not longer than 2.5–4 cm (1–1½ inches) and not wider at the head than 1–2.5 cm (½–1 inch), I find that the best way is to take each large floweret and begin by slicing the stems crosswise into fairly thin rounds. Keep these, as they are quite edible. When you reach the upper end of the stem, start breaking off the small flowerets. Slice the stem into rounds whenever it seems too long, and keep the rounds. Wash the flowerets and the stem rounds in a colander and leave to drain.

Heat oil in 25–30 cm (10–12 inch) frying-pan over medium heat. Add the ginger paste and turmeric. Fry, stirring constantly; after about 2 minutes, add green chilli or cayenne and green coriander; after another 2 minutes, put in the cauliflower, continuing to cook and stir for 5 minutes. (If necessary, add 1 tsp warm water at a time to prevent sticking.) Now add the cumin, coriander, garam masala, lemon juice, salt and 3 tbsp warm water, cook and stir for about 5 minutes, then cover, lower flame, and let cook slowly for 35 to 45 minutes (the tightly packed cauliflower takes longer to cook), stirring gently every 10 minutes. The cauliflower is done when it is tender with just a faint trace of crispness along its inner spine.

To serve: Lift out gently and place in serving dish – a low, wide bowl would be best. Serve with hot chapatis, pooris, or parathas, or serve with any kind of lentils and plain boiled rice.

Cauliflower with onion and tomato

Serves 6–8

---

1 medium-sized onion, peeled and coarsely chopped	1 medium-sized fresh or tinned tomato, peeled and chopped
4 cloves garlic, peeled and coarsely chopped	1 tbsp chopped fresh green coriander
a piece of fresh ginger, 5 cm (2 inches) long and 2.5 cm (1 inch) wide, peeled and coarsely chopped	1 fresh hot green chilli, washed and finely sliced or 1/4 tsp cayenne pepper (optional)
1 large head fresh cauliflower, or 2 small ones	2 tsp ground coriander
	1 tsp ground cumin
8 tbsp vegetable oil	1 tsp garam masala
1/2 tsp ground turmeric	2 tsp salt
	1 tbsp lemon juice

Put chopped onion, garlic and ginger in blender with 4 tbsp of water and blend to a paste.

Break off cauliflower into small flowerets (see preceding recipe), not longer than 2.5-4 cm (1–1½ inches), and not wider at the head than 1–2.5 cm (½–1 inch). Wash in colander and leave to drain.

Heat the oil in a heavy-bottomed 25–30 cm (10–12 inch) pot over medium flame, pour in the paste from the blender, and add the turmeric. Fry, stirring, for 5 minutes.

Add the chopped tomato, green coriander and green chilli or cayenne, and fry for 5 minutes. If necessary, add 1 tsp of warm water at a time and stir to prevent sticking. Now put in the cauliflower, coriander, cumin, garam masala, salt and lemon juice. Stir for a minute. Add 4 tbsp warm water, stir, cover, lower flame, and allow to cook slowly for 35 to 45 minutes (the tightly packed cauliflower heads take longer to cook). Stir gently every 10 minutes or so. The cauliflower is done when each floweret is tender with just a faint trace of crispness along its inner spine.

To serve: Follow suggestions of previous recipe.

Courgettes with onions, tomato and cumin

Serves 6

---

2 medium-sized onions	about 1½ tsp salt
3 largish courgettes, about 1.25 kg	¹/₁₆ tsp freshly ground black pepper
(2½ lb)	1½ tbsp lemon juice
4 tbsp vegetable oil	¹/₁₆–¹/₈ tsp cayenne pepper (optional)
1 tsp whole cumin seeds	4 tbsp finely chopped fresh green
1 large tomato about 225 g (8 oz),	coriander, or parsley
peeled and chopped	

Peel the onions, cut in half lengthwise, then slice into fine half rings. Trim the ends off the courgettes, then quarter them lengthwise. Cut away the seeded section and then cut crosswise into 1–2 cm (½–¾ inch) sections.

Heat the oil in a large frying pan over a medium flame. When hot, put in the whole cumin seeds. As soon as they turn a few shades darker (this takes just a few seconds) put in the onions. Turn heat to medium and sauté onions for about 2 minutes. Add the tomatoes and stir for a few seconds. Now cover, lower heat, and let onions and tomatoes cook for 10 minutes. Lift cover and gently mash down the tomato pieces. Add the courgettes and 1¼ tsp salt (add the other ¼ tsp salt towards the end if you think you need it). Stir and fry for another 2 minutes on medium heat.

Add 2 tbsp water, cover immediately with a well-fitting lid, turn heat down and steam gently for 4 to 6 minutes or until the courgettes are tender but still retain some crispness. (Young courgettes will cook much faster.) Lift cover, and add black pepper, lemon juice, cayenne pepper and chopped coriander. Mix and taste for salt-sour balance. Cover and steam for another minute. Serve either hot or cold on a bed of lettuce leaves as a salad.

Courgette 'meatballs'

Makes 16 'meatballs' and serves 4–6 people

An exquisitely elegant dish, it consists of tender 'meatballs' made out of grated courgette, bathed in a creamy, spicy sauce. In India, a long green marrow, shaped rather like a bowling pin, is used for this dish. If you can find such a marrow in a Chinese or Indian grocery store, do use it. It needs to be peeled and seeded before it is grated. If you cannot find it, courgettes make an excellent substitute.

For the 'meatballs'
3 medium-sized courgettes, about 450-600 g (1–1¼ lb)
½ tsp salt
about 1 fresh hot green chilli, finely chopped
3 tbsp finely chopped onion
½ tsp peeled and very finely grated fresh ginger
2 tbsp finely chopped fresh green coriander
45 g (1½ oz) gram flour
vegetable oil for deep frying

For the sauce
5 tbsp vegetable oil for deep frying
2 medium-sized onions, peeled and very finely chopped
¼ tsp ground turmeric
¹⁄₁₆ tsp cayenne pepper
1 tsp ground cumin seeds
2 tsp ground coriander seeds
225 g (8 oz) tomatoes (about 2 tomatoes), peeled and finely chopped
250 ml (8 fl oz) single cream
½ tsp garam masala
½ tsp ground roasted cumin seeds
¼–⅓ tsp salt

Wash, trim and grate the courgettes. Put them into a bowl and sprinkle them with the ½ tsp salt. Set them aside for half an hour.

Squeeze as much liquid as possible out of the courgettes by pressing handfuls between your two palms. Save this courgette liquid for the sauce. Dry off the bowl and put the courgettes back in it. Add the chopped chilli (you may want to use more than 1 chilli, depending on your taste), the 3 tbsp chopped onion, the grated ginger and the fresh coriander. Sift the gram flour over this vegetable mixture. Mix well and form 16 neat balls.

In a frying pan, wok, or other utensil for deep frying, heat about 4 cm (1½ inches) of oil over a medium flame (a wok should have 4 cm (1½ inches) at its centre). When hot, put in 5 to 6 of the balls, or as many as the utensil will hold easily in one layer. Fry for about 1½ minutes, or until the balls turn a rich, reddish-brown colour. Turn the balls every now and then as they fry. Remove them with a slotted spoon when they are done and leave to drain on a plate lined with kitchen paper. Do all the 'meatballs' this way.

To make the sauce, remove 5 tbsp of the oil used in deep frying and put this in a 25 cm (10 inch) frying or sauté pan. Heat the oil over a medium flame. When hot, put in the finely chopped onions. Stir and fry for 7 to 8 minutes or until the onions begin to turn brown at the edges. Take the pan off the fire for a couple of seconds and add the turmeric, cayenne, ground cumin and ground coriander. Stir once and put the pan back on the fire. Stir for another 5 seconds and then add the chopped tomatoes. Stir and fry on medium heat for 5 minutes. Add the courgette juice. (You need 250 ml (8 fl oz), if you have less, add some water.) Bring to the boil. Cover, lower heat and let the sauce simmer gently for 15 minutes. (This much of the recipe may be prepared several hours ahead of time.) Add the cream, garam masala, ground roasted cumin and the 1/4–1/3 tsp salt. Mix well, bring to a simmer and cook for 1 minute. Now put in the 'meatballs'. Spoon the sauce over them. Cover, and simmer very gently for 6 to 7 minutes. Spoon the sauce over the 'meatballs' a few times during this cooking period.

These 'meatballs' turn very soft when cooked in the sauce, so handle them gently and serve immediately.

Mushrooms with cumin and asafetida

Serves 4–6

---

675 g (1 1/2 lb) fresh mushrooms
2 tbsp vegetable oil
a generous pinch ground asafetida, or 3 mm (1/8 inch) lump asafetida
1/2 tsp whole cumin seeds

2 whole hot dried red peppers
1/4 tsp ground turmeric
300 ml (1/2 pint) tomato sauce (see page 114)
1 tsp salt

Clean mushrooms. Chop off the coarse stem ends.
Heat oil in 2.3–3.4 litre (4–6 pint) pot over medium heat, and put in the asafetida. It will sizzle and expand within 5 seconds. Now add the cumin seeds, and as soon as they darken (5 to 10 seconds), the red peppers. Stir

once and add the turmeric and the mushrooms. Stir mushrooms for ½ minute and add the tomato sauce, 600 ml (1 pint) of water and the salt. Cover, lower heat, and simmer gently for 15 to 20 minutes.

Remove from heat. The mushrooms can be eaten now, but it is better to let them sit for 1 to 2 hours to absorb the taste of the broth-like sauce, and then reheat.

To serve: Serve in little individual bowls. The thin, delicious sauce can be eaten with a spoon or with hot chapatis or pooris. You can easily build a meal around the mushrooms.

Mushrooms with onion, garlic and ginger

Serves 4

This is really my mother's recipe, which I have acquired via my sister-in-law. It is very simple – and good.

---

340 g (12 oz) medium-sized mushrooms
a 2.5 cm (1 inch) cube of fresh ginger, peeled and finely grated
6 cloves garlic, peeled and mashed to a pulp or grated
4 tbsp vegetable oil

1 medium-sized onion, peeled and very finely chopped
¼ tsp ground turmeric
⅛ tsp cayenne pepper, or more to taste
½–¾ tsp salt

Wipe the mushrooms with a damp cloth and then halve them. Combine the ginger and garlic in a small cup with 3 tbsp water.

Heat the oil in an 18 cm (7 inch) wide pot over a medium-high flame. When hot, put in the chopped onion and fry, stirring, for about 2 minutes or until onion is a golden-brown colour. Add the ginger-garlic paste. Keep stirring and frying for another 2 minutes. If the water evaporates, sprinkle a little more in (about 2 tsp). Now add the turmeric and cayenne. Stir for a second. Add the mushrooms, ½ tsp salt and 100 ml (4 fl oz) water. Stir, and bring to a simmer. Cover, lower heat, and simmer gently for 10 minutes. Check the salt. You may wish to add a bit more. Stir. Serve with an Indian bread or a rice dish.

Whole okra

Serves 6

---

675 g (1½ lb) fresh, tender okra
6 tbsp vegetable oil
2 medium-sized onions, peeled and
finely chopped
6 cloves garlic, peeled and finely
chopped

½ tsp ground turmeric
1¼–1½ tsp salt
⅛ tsp freshly ground black pepper
1/16–⅛ tsp cayenne pepper
(optional)

Wash okra and trim it. (To trim whole okra, cut off a small section at the tip. The stem end looks prettiest if trimmed in a conical shape.)

Heat oil in a 25–30 cm (10–12 inch) frying-pan over a medium flame. Add the onions and garlic and fry, stirring frequently, for 5 minutes. Add okra and fry for another 5 minutes. Now put in the turmeric, salt, black pepper, cayenne and 50 ml (2 fl oz) water. Stir well to mix. Cover tightly, lower heat, and steam gently for about 15 to 20 minutes or until okra is tender. (Larger pods will take a bit longer to cook through.) Stir very gently every 5 minutes, replacing the lid each time. If any extra liquid remains in the frying pan, it should be boiled away so okra has a 'dry' look.

Okra with onions

Serves 4–6

This is the way okra is generally cooked in most parts of Delhi. The success of this dish depends upon the onion paste being cooked to the right consistency before the okra is added.

---

4 medium-sized onions, peeled and
coarsely chopped
5 cloves of garlic, peeled and
coarsely chopped
a piece of fresh ginger, about 5 cm
(2 inches) long, 2.5 cm (1 inch)
thick, and 2.5 cm (1 inch) wide,
peeled and coarsely chopped
6 tbsp vegetable oil
1 tsp whole cumin seeds

2 tsp whole fennel seeds
1 tsp ground turmeric
1 tbsp ground coriander
1 tbsp tomato purée
450 g (1 lb) fresh young okra
1 tsp salt
2 tsp garam masala
2 tbsp lemon juice
¼ tsp cayenne pepper (optional)

Put onion, garlic and ginger in electric blender, add 50 ml (2 fl oz) warm water, and blend to a paste.

Heat oil in a 25–30 cm (10–12 inch) frying-pan over medium heat. Add the cumin and fennel seeds. When the fennel begins to change colour (20 seconds or so), add the paste from the blender and the turmeric.

Cook this paste over medium heat for about 20 minutes, stirring frequently and scraping the bottom. The paste will reduce and turn a lovely brown colour.

Add the coriander and fry, stirring; after a minute, add the tomato purée and cook, stirring, for about 1 minute. Turn off the heat under the frying-pan.

Wash the okra and wipe it with a paper towel. Slice a few pods at a time into 0.5 cm (1/4 inch) rounds.

Turn the heat to medium again under the frying-pan with the onion paste. Add the okra, salt, garam masala, lemon juice and 100 ml (4 fl oz) of warm water. When the onion paste starts bubbling, cover, turn heat very low, and allow to cook slowly for 35 minutes, or until tender. Stir every 10 minutes or so to prevent sticking.

To serve: Serve like stuffed okra, the next recipe.

Stuffed whole okra

Serves 4–6

---

8 medium-sized onions, peeled and finely chopped	4 tsp whole fennel seeds
	20 whole fenugreek seeds
8 cloves garlic, peeled and minced	10 tbsp vegetable oil
a piece of fresh ginger, about 5 cm (2 inches) by 4 cm (1½ inches) by 2.5 cm (1 inch), peeled and grated	1 tsp ground turmeric
	salt
	4 tsp garam masala
	2 tbsp lemon juice
2 tsp whole cumin seeds	450 g (1 lb) fresh young okra

The stuffing: Since this dish is to be cooked in two 25 cm (10 inch) frying-pans to accommodate all the okra, divide the onions, garlic and ginger into two equal piles. Make two separate equal piles of the cumin, fennel and fenugreek seeds.

Heat 5 tbsp of oil in each frying-pan over medium heat, and when hot, put in the cumin, fennel and fenugreek seeds. As they begin to pop and change colour (5 to 10 seconds), put half the onion, garlic and ginger and 1/2 tsp turmeric into each frying-pan. Stir and fry over medium heat for about 10–12 minutes until the onions look a rich brown. Stir frequently.

Add 1/2 tsp salt and 1 tsp garam masala to each frying-pan and stir. Turn off heat under both frying-pans. Using a slotted spoon, remove onion mixture from frying-pans, leaving as much of the cooking fat behind as possible. You will need it later. Collect the onion mixture from both frying-pans in a bowl, add 2 more tsp garam masala and the lemon juice, mix, and set aside to cool.

The okra: Wash the okra and pat it dry with paper towels. Trim off the head and the lower tip.

Since the stuffing of the okra takes a little time, place the okra, the bowl of stuffing, a clean platter, and a small sharp knife on a table, and settle yourself on a chair. Pick up one okra pod at a time. Make a slit along its length, being sure that you do *not* go through the opposite side and that you leave about 3 mm (1/8 inch) at the top and bottom unslit.

Assuming you are right-handed, slip your left thumb into the pod to keep the slit open. With your right thumb and fingers, pick up a little stuffing at a time and push it into the slit. You will need from 1/4 to 1 tsp of stuffing for each pod, depending on its size. As each pod is stuffed, set it aside on the platter.

Turn on the flame under both frying-pans and keep on medium-low heat. Divide the okra between the two frying-pans and lay them slit side up in the pans in a single layer if possible (a few overlapping won't matter). Cook for 5 minutes, shake salt (about 1/4 tsp to each pan) over okra, add 2 tbsp warm water to each pan, cover, lower flames to very, very low, and cook gently for 30 minutes or until the okra is tender.

To serve: Lift out gently and arrange on warm platter. Serve with Rice with Peas, Pork Chops à la Jaffrey, and Potatoes with Asafetida and Cumin. It also goes very well with all Indian breads.

Pyazwale sookhe aloo ('dry' potatoes with onions)

Serves 6–8

Here is another simple potato dish that can be served as a vegetable with pooris or as an appetizer, on top of savoury biscuits.

---

6 medium-sized potatoes
5 tbsp vegetable oil
1/8 tsp ground asafetida, or 3 mm
   (1/8 inch) lump asafetida
1/2 tsp whole cumin seeds
2 1/2 tsp whole black mustard seeds
1-3 whole dried red peppers
   (optional – 1 red pepper will
   make it mildly hot; 3 very hot)

1 medium-sized onion, peeled and
   coarsely chopped
1/2 tsp ground turmeric
1 1/4 tsp salt
1 tsp garam masala
2 tbsp lemon juice

Boil the potatoes in their jackets. Peel them and mash them coarsely with a fork or hand masher.

Heat the oil in a 25–30 cm (10–12 inch) frying-pan over medium heat. When hot, first put in it the asafetida; after it has sizzled for a few seconds, add the cumin and mustard seeds; then in 10 seconds or so, the red pepper (or peppers). When pepper changes colour (1 to 5 seconds), put in the chopped onions and turmeric. After the onions have cooked for 3 to 5 minutes and turned brown at the edges, put in the mashed potatoes, salt, garam masala and lemon juice. Fry, stirring and mixing, for 5 to 7 minutes.

To serve: Place in a warmed dish and serve with chapatis, pooris, or parathas. This is a good dish to take on picnics, too. Serve as an appetizer on top of Melba toast or savoury biscuits. (Remove whole red peppers before placing on any kind of toast.)

Potatoes with asafetida and cumin

Serves 4–5

This was one of the most popular potato dishes in our family. It is a 'wet' dish and needs to be served in small individual bowls. It is very good – and easy to make.

4–5 medium-sized potatoes
2 tbsp vegetable oil
1/8 tsp ground asafetida, or 3 mm (1/8 inch) lump asafetida
1/2 tsp whole cumin seeds

1–2 dried hot red peppers (optional)
1/2 tsp turmeric
350 ml (12 fl oz) tomato sauce (see page 114)
1 tsp salt

Wash, peel and quarter potatoes. Put them in bowl with cold water to cover.

In 2.3–3.4 litre (4–6 pint) pot, heat oil over medium heat. As it heats, put potatoes in colander to drain. When the fat is hot, put in the asafetida; after it sizzles (5 seconds), add the cumin seeds; when they sizzle and change colour (5 to 10 seconds), add the red peppers, which will begin to change colour in a couple of seconds. Now put in the drained potatoes and the turmeric. Fry the potatoes for about 2 minutes, stirring them now and then.

Now put in 450 ml (3/4 pint) water, tomato sauce and salt. Bring to the boil. Cover and allow to simmer very gently for about 1 1/2 hours.

To serve: Take to the table in a deep dish. Give each person a little bowl in which to put the potatoes as well as the sauce. These potatoes are best served with pooris, chapatis, or parathas, but they are also good with plain boiled rice and Lamb with Onions and Mushrooms. Left-overs can be put in the blender or mashed to make an excellent soup.

Maya's potatoes

Serves 6–8

My sister-in-law makes this dish, so I've named it after her. In India, we take it with us on picnics, heat it on a portable charcoal stove, and eat it with 'stale' pooris and hot mango pickle.

8 medium-sized potatoes
oil for deep frying
1 onion, peeled and coarsely
   chopped
4 garlic cloves, peeled and coarsely
   chopped
6 tbsp oil (or re-use 6 tbsp strained
   deep-frying fat)
asafetida (optional), 3 mm (1/8 inch)
   square piece or 1 large pinch
   ground
7 fenugreek seeds

1/2 tsp fennel seeds
1/4 tsp black onion seeds (kalonji), if
   available
1/4 tsp black mustard seeds
1 bay leaf
3 dried hot red peppers (optional, or
   use less)
1/2 tsp ground turmeric
2 medium-sized tomatoes (tinned or
   fresh), peeled and chopped
1 pinch sugar
1 1/2 tsp salt

Boil potatoes, preferably 2 hours ahead, and leave to cool. Just before you begin cooking, peel the potatoes and halve them; quarter them if they are large.

Heat over medium flame 2.5–5 cm (1–2 inches) of oil in 2.5–30 cm (10–12 inch) frying-pan, wok or *karhai*, and fry the potatoes in two or three batches until golden-brown on all sides. (If you prefer, you can fry the potatoes in much shallower fat. Just make sure you get them lightly browned on all sides.) Drain and set aside.

Put the chopped onion and garlic into blender with 3 tablespoons water and blend to a paste.

Heat 6 tbsp of oil in a heavy-bottomed 25–30 cm (10–12 inch) pot. Keep heat on medium. When very hot, add asafetida, fenugreek seeds, fennel seeds, onion seeds, mustard seeds, bay leaf and red peppers in this order and in quick succession. Fry 10 to 20 seconds, until bay leaf and peppers begin to turn dark. Add paste from blender and turmeric, and fry, stirring, for 5 minutes; then add chopped tomatoes and sugar and cook another 5 minutes. Stir in gently 600 ml (1 pint) water, salt and fried potatoes, and bring to boil. Cover, lower flame, and simmer for 10 minutes. Raise cover, gently lift each potato and turn it over, cover, and simmer for another 10 minutes.

To serve: Place potatoes gently in a shallow serving dish. Pour the sauce over them and serve with pooris or parathas. For a simple meal try Kheema with Fried Onions, chapatis, and this potato dish.

Diced potatoes with spinach

Serves 6

All over North India, potatoes are cooked with greens. Fenugreek greens are preferred, but spinach makes a good alternative.

5-6 medium-sized waxy potatoes,
about 900 g (2 lb)
1 tbsp plus 1 tsp salt
450 g (1 lb) fresh or 1 packet frozen
leaf spinach
6 tbsp vegetable oil or ghee
1/2 tsp whole black mustard seeds

1 large onion, 85–100 g (3–3 1/2 oz),
peeled and chopped
2 cloves garlic, peeled and finely
chopped
1 tsp garam masala
1/16-1/8 tsp cayenne pepper (optional)

Bring 1.4 litres (2 1/2 pints) of water to the boil. Peel potatoes and dice into 2 cm (3/4 inch) cubes, then add to boiling water with 1 tbsp salt. Bring to the boil again. Cover, turn heat to low and cook potatoes until they are just tender – about 6 minutes. Do not overcook. Drain. Spread potatoes out and leave to cool.

If using fresh spinach, wash carefully and drop into large pan of boiling water to wilt. Drain. Squeeze out as much liquid as possible from spinach and chop finely. If using frozen leaf spinach, cook according to instructions. Drain, squeeze out liquid, and chop. Set aside.

Heat oil in a heavy, 30 cm (12 inch), preferably nonstick frying-pan over a medium-high flame. When very hot, put in the mustard seeds. As soon as the seeds begin to pop (this just takes a few seconds), add the onion and garlic. Turn heat to medium and fry for 3 to 4 minutes. The onions should turn very lightly brown at the edges. Now put in the chopped spinach and keep stirring and frying for another 10 minutes.

Add the cooked potatoes, 1 tsp salt, the garam masala and the cayenne pepper. Stir and mix gently until potatoes are heated through.

Potato patties (aloo-ki-tikiya)

12 patties

These delicious patties are sold on street corners in India pretty much the way chestnuts are sold here. Eaten as snacks or with meals, they consist of mashed potatoes stuffed with lentils and spices.

6 medium-sized potatoes	5 fenugreek seeds
3 tbsp yellow split peas, soaked overnight in 300 ml (1/2 pint) cold water and 1/2 tsp salt	2 tbsp chopped onion
	3 tbsp trimmed, chopped fresh green coriander
3 tsp salt	1/2-1 fresh hot green chilli, finely sliced (optional)
2 tbsp vegetable oil plus oil for frying patties	

Two hours before dinner, boil the potatoes in their jackets. While potatoes are boiling, drain split peas. Then boil them in a 1.1–2.3 litre (2–4 pint) pot with 600 ml (1 pint) cold water and 1/2 tsp salt for 15 minutes. Remove from heat and drain in a colander or strainer, shaking it to get out as much water as you can, and invert peas in bowl. Cover the bowl.

In a frying-pan heat 2 tbsp oil over a medium flame. When very hot, add the fenugreek seeds, and when they begin to change colour (5 to 10 seconds), put in the onions, continuing to fry about 2 minutes until the onions begin to turn brown at the edges. Add the green coriander and green chilli, and stir another 2 to 3 minutes. Next, put in the drained split peas and 1/2 tsp salt. Keep stirring and cook for about 5 minutes, until all the water has evaporated and the mixture in the frying-pan seems to become one lump. Cover and set aside.

Peel and mash potatoes with a fork or hand masher. (Do not use a whipping gadget or an electric mixer. Don't add butter.) A few lumps will remain, but don't worry – just get the potatoes as smooth as you can. Add 2 tsp salt and mix thoroughly.

To form patties: Divide the mashed potatoes into 12 balls. Divide the split pea mixture into 12 portions. Flatten each potato ball on the palm of your hand, put a portion of the split pea stuffing in the centre of it, and cover the stuffing with the mashed potato by bringing the outer circumference to the centre. Make a ball again. Flatten it gently to have a patty about 7.5 cm (3 inches) in diameter. Make all the patties this way, keeping them covered on a platter if you are not going to be eating soon. (You can prepare this much of the recipe from a few hours to a day ahead.)

Cooking these patties is an art in itself. In India they are cooked on a *tava*, a large, slightly curved iron plate. If you have a *tava*, it is really the ideal utensil to use. If you don't, use a heavy-bottomed frying-pan, but remember to cook only two or three patties at a time. If you crowd them it becomes difficult to lift and turn them.

Since these patties are cooked like pancakes with very little oil, use only enough to coat the bottom of your frying-pan or *tava*, and heat over medium-low flame. Put in a few potato patties and cook them slowly – about 8 to 10 minutes on each side. When one side turns a golden-red, carefully work your spatula under it without breaking the hard crust and drop it over on its unfried side. Add another teaspoon of oil, swirling it around. Fry this side for 8 to 10 minutes also, until it has formed a red-brown crust. If the patties brown too quickly, lower the heat.

Note: Since these have to be served hot, and since you may not be able to make many at a time in a frying-pan, you could use two frying-pans.

To serve: Place on a heated platter and serve hot. These patties are marvellous for snacks. They are usually served with Fresh Green Chutney with Coriander Leaves and Yogurt.

Or you could serve them as part of any meal. I once cooked a rather pleasant lunch of chicken breasts grilled with just butter, salt, pepper and lemon. I also made a simple green salad and we had these potato patties. It was wonderful!

Tomato sauce

Tomato sauce is used in some of my recipes. This is how you can make it:

Take a 400 g (14 oz) tin of tomatoes and pour the contents into a stainless steel pot or a pot lined with a non-metallic substance. Add ¼ tsp salt and ¼ tsp sugar. Bring to the boil. Cook on medium heat, stirring frequently and breaking up the tomatoes, until you reduce contents of pot by half. Pour these contents into an electric blender and blend until you have a smooth paste. A 400 g (14 oz) tin of tomatoes should yield 250–300 ml (8–10 fl oz) of sauce. The sauce can be frozen or kept covered in the refrigerator for at least a week.

RICE

The statistics astonish me. They say an average Indian eats 225 to 300 grams (one-half to two-thirds of a pound) of rice per day whereas the Englishman eats, on an average, about two kilograms (four pounds) of rice per year! The English, on the whole, have really not discovered rice. They dismiss rice as a 'starch' and as a poor relative of the more popular 'starches' – potatoes and pasta. Potatoes can be baked, fried, mashed, boiled, 'duchessed', varied ad infinitum, and there are so many different kinds of pasta . . . But rice? What can you do with rice? So even when it *is* served here, more often than not it is cooked unimaginatively and amateurishly.

Let us start at the very beginning. What kind of rice should you buy? Looking at the varieties available in the average supermarket, I can more easily tell you what not to buy. Don't buy quick-cooking or 'instant' rice. Don't buy parboiled or partially cooked rice. Neither of them really tastes like rice. Also, don't buy prepackaged mixes with herbs and spices. There is no 'mix' that you cannot manage better on your own. Once you understand and master the different methods of cooking rice, there is no limit to the number of recipes you can invent.

Buy a long-grain uncooked rice. Patna rice is good and easily available. If you are lucky enough to be near a delicatessen carrying basmati rice do buy it. This rice is grown in the foothills of the Himalayas. It has a narrow, long grain and a very special flavour and smell.

For most of the recipes in this book, I have used long-grain rice. If you use some other variety, you may have to experiment with the amount of water needed and the cooking time. All uncooked rices are not the same. Where I have used Indian basmati rice, I have indicated how it should be cooked.

Most Indians eat rice with their hands. It is mixed with the lentils or meat and vegetables and eaten with the tips of the fingers. Not all the rice is mixed with the rest of the food at once. You serve yourself each dish on a separate part of your plate. The only things you may put on top of your rice are the lentils and other soup-like and semi-liquid dishes.

Rice can be cooked with almost any meat, vegetable or fish and served as a main dish. It can be cooked with whole or powdered spices; it can be boiled, steamed or baked; it can be cooked in water or in aromatic broths. It can be the side dish as in plain boiled rice, or it can be the main course as in pullao and biryani. It can be pounded or ground to make desserts like *kheer* and *phirni*.

For important occasions, rice is tinted a bright yellow with turmeric or vegetable colouring or, best of all, with saffron, which gives it not just a yellowish-orange saffron colour but a delicious fragrance as well. I'll never forget my first introduction to saffron. I was in my early teens and on my first visit to Kashmir. We were riding past a hill and valley that were completely purple from all the crocuses growing there. I remarked on their beauty to my Kashmiri companions, who in turn told me that the flowers meant something more than just beauty to them. 'This is *zaafraan*,' they said. *Zaafraan*? I thought. I wondered vaguely why, if this was the saffron flower, it was not saffron-coloured. One of the young Kashmiri boys got off his horse, plucked a flower, and brought it to me. He pulled its petals apart, showing me the stigma, which is dried and called saffron, and he told me that thousands of stigmas were needed to get a tablespoon of saffron.

Rice is not used merely for eating, though. It has its place in all the Hindu religious ceremonies; it is thrown into the fire at weddings because it is the great symbol of fertility. My family priest explained it to me this way: 'A young girl is like a rice plant. The rice is planted in one field, but it cannot bear fruit until it is transplanted into another field. So it is with the girl. She is born in her father's house, but she cannot bear children until she is transplanted into her husband's house.'

Plain boiled rice

Serves 4–6

340 g (12 oz) long-grain rice	1 tbsp butter
750 ml (1¼ pints) water	1 tsp salt

Combine all the ingredients in a 2.3–3.4 litre (4–6 pint) heavy-bottomed pot with tight-fitting lid. Bring to the boil, cover, and turn flame as low as it will go. Leave for 25 to 30 minutes. Lift cover and quickly check to see if rice is cooked through. Turn off heat, and leave lid on until ready to serve.

(When cooking plain boiled rice, I always cook more than I need because there are such wonderful ways of dressing up cooked rice. I cover and refrigerate the left-overs, and cook them for breakfast, lunch or dinner.)

Plain baked rice

Serves 6

340 g (12 oz) long-grain rice	4 tbsp butter
1 tbsp salt	

Preheat oven to 150°C (300°F) mark 2.

Fill a 3.4 litre (6 pint) pot with about 2.8 litres (5 pints) of water, add the salt, and set over a high flame.

Meanwhile, wash and drain the rice in a colander.

When the water is boiling, put the rice in it. Bring to a second boil, and boil rapidly for exactly 5 minutes.

Drain the rice by pouring it through a colander.

Put the rice in an ovenproof dish. Cut the butter into 4 patties and place over the rice. Now cut a piece of aluminium foil 5 cm (2 inches) larger than the rim of the dish, cover the dish, and then put the lid on top of the foil. Crinkle foil around the edges to seal as thoroughly as possible. The rice has to cook in its own steam, so that steam must not be allowed to escape.

Place dish in oven for 45 to 50 minutes (check after 45 minutes to see whether rice is done).

Plain basmati rice

Serves 6

---

340 g (12 oz) basmati rice	**1 tbsp butter**
1¼ tsp salt	

Wash the rice well in cold water. Soak it in a bowl with 1.1 litres (2 pints) of water and ½ tsp salt for 30 minutes. Then drain.

Melt the butter in a heavy-bottomed pot over medium flame. Pour in the drained rice and stir for a minute. Add 550 ml (18 fl oz) water and ¾ tsp salt. Bring to the boil, cover, lower heat to *very* low, and cook for 20 minutes.

Lift lid. Mix rice gently with fork. Cover again and cook for another 10 minutes, or until rice is tender.

Serve with almost any dish you like. I love it with Moong Dal, Pyazwala Khare Masale Ka Gosht, lime wedges and a cucumber relish of some kind.

Basmati rice with spices and saffron

Serves 6

Even though this recipe is for Indian basmati rice, any long-grain, fine-quality rice can be used instead.

---

1 tsp leaf saffron, loosely packed, roasted and crumbled	**1¼ tsp salt**
2 tbsp warm milk	**2 tbsp vegetable oil**
340 g (12 oz) basmati or long-grain rice	**5 cardamom pods**
	2 cinnamon sticks, 6.5–7.5 cm (2½–3 inches) long

In a small container, soak saffron in warm milk.

Wash the rice well in cold water. Soak it in a bowl with 1.1 litres (2 pints) water and ½ tsp salt for 30 minutes, then drain.

Heat the oil over medium flame in 2.3–3.4 litre (4–6 pint) heavy-bottomed pot (with a tight-fitting lid – to be used later), put in the cardamom pods and cinnamon sticks, and stir a few times. Add the rice, frying and stirring for about a minute.

Add 550 ml (18 fl oz) water and ³/₄ tsp salt. Bring to the boil, cover, reduce heat to *very* low, and cook for 20 minutes.

Lift off cover. Gently but quickly mix rice with a fork, turning it around a bit. Pour the saffron milk in 2 or 3 streaks over the rice. Cover and keep cooking for another 10 minutes or until rice is quite done.

To serve: Turn the rice onto a platter with a fork (this keeps the grains whole). Serve with Chicken Moghlai and Yogurt with Spinach.

Sweet rice

Serves 6

This is a very simple recipe for sweet rice. It goes rather well with many English dishes, like baked ham, pork chops, roast loin of pork, lamb chops, etc. It is mild flavoured and not too sweet. If you like, you could elaborate on the recipe by adding nuts and raisins.

2¹/₂ tbsp vegetable oil
4 whole cloves
3–4 whole cardamom pods
4 black peppercorns
1 bay leaf
1 medium-sized onion, peeled and
    sliced into fine rings
340 g (12 oz) long-grain rice
1 tbsp ground coriander

¹/₂ tsp ground cinnamon
¹/₄ tsp ground nutmeg
750 ml (1¹/₄ pints) homemade beef
    or lamb stock or tinned beef
    broth (not bouillon)
¹/₂ tsp salt (more if broth is
    unsalted)
1 tbsp granulated brown sugar

Over a medium flame, heat the oil in a 2.3 litre (4 pint) heavy-bottomed pot (with a tight-fitting lid – to be used later). When very hot, add the cloves and cardamom pods, peppercorns and bay leaf. Fry for about 5 seconds, until the spices begin to expand and change colour. Now add the onion rings and fry for about 3 to 5 minutes, until the onions turn light brown with darkish edges. Put in the rice, coriander, cinnamon and nutmeg, and stir for 5 minutes.

Next, pour in the broth and salt, stir, cover, and turn the flame very low. Let cook for about 15 minutes.

Lift the lid, put in the brown sugar, and stir quickly with a fork. Cover again and cook for another 15 to 20 minutes.

To serve: Serve plain, or garnished with slivered almonds.

Rice with whole spices

Serves 6

Rice is cooked with whole cinnamon sticks, bay leaves, cloves, black peppers and cardamom pods. It is a very light and fragrant dish – and easy to make.

---

1 medium-sized onion	2 cinnamon sticks, about 7.5 cm
2 tbsp vegetable oil	(3 inches) long
6 whole cloves	3 bay leaves
10 black peppercorns	340 g (12 oz) long-grain rice
5 cardamom pods	1 tsp salt

Peel onion and slice into fine rounds. Halve the rounds.

Heat the oil in a 3.4 litre (6 pint) heavy-bottomed pot (with tight-fitting lid – to be used later) over medium heat, put in the onions, and fry, stirring, until they are brown and crisp (but *not* burned) – about 8 to 10 minutes. With a slotted spoon, remove the onions and leave them on a paper towel to drain.

In the same fat, fry the cloves, peppercorns, cardamom pods, cinnamon sticks and bay leaves for 10 to 20 seconds or until spices begin to expand and change colour. Add the rice, and fry, stirring, for another minute or two. Now put in 750 ml (1¼ pints) water and the salt. Bring to the boil, cover, and reduce heat to very low. Cook 25 to 35 minutes, until done. Halfway through the cooking, stir once gently with a fork.

To serve: Spoon out the rice onto a warm platter, breaking any lumps with the back of a slotted spoon. The whole spices serve as a garnish – just warn your family or guests not to bite into them. Sprinkle fried onions over rice.

Serve with baked fish and almost any meat or chicken dish.

Rice with potatoes and cumin seed

Serves 6

Rice *and* potatoes? A double starch? It's not really all *that* frightening. After all, if you were going to serve yourself a spoonful of rice, you could just as easily serve yourself a spoonful of rice *and* potatoes. The starch content is about the same, whether you're eating one starch or two, and in Britain at least the combination has the virtue of novelty.

---

2 medium-sized or 1 large potato
4 tbsp vegetable oil
1/2 tbsp whole cumin seeds

340 g (12 oz) long-grain rice
1 tsp salt

Peel potato, and dice into 2 cm (3/4 inch) cubes.

Heat oil in a heavy-bottomed pot (with tight-fitting lid – to be used later) over medium heat. When very hot, add the cumin seeds, and after they have begun to change colour and 'pop' (about 10 to 20 seconds), put in the potatoes. Let the potatoes brown to a nice golden colour on all sides. Then add the rice and stir for about 2 minutes. Add 750 ml (1 1/4 pints) water and salt, stir, and bring to the boil. Cover, turn the flame very low, and cook for 25 to 30 minutes. See if rice is done; if not, stir and cook for another 5 minutes.

To serve: Serve with marinated pork chops – or with Kheema and green beans. This is a simple yet very versatile dish that could be served with plain yogurt to an invalid or with Korma at a banquet.

Rice with cauliflower and cumin seed

Serves 6

This dish is very much like the preceding one, only cauliflower is substituted for the potatoes.

---

1 small head cauliflower	2¹/₂ tbsp vegetable oil
vegetable oil (enough to have about 4 cm (1¹/₂ inches) in cauliflower frying-pan)	¹/₂ tsp whole cumin seeds
	340 g (12 oz) long-grain rice
freshly ground pepper	salt

Break cauliflower into flowerets not bigger than 4 cm (1¹/₂ inches) in length and 2.5 cm (1 inch) in width at the head. Wash and drain flowerets thoroughly on paper towels.

Heat enough oil in frying-pan, wok or *karhai* to have about 4 cm (1¹/₂ inches). Keep on medium flame, much as you would for potato-chips. When hot, put in the flowerets a batch at a time and deep-fry until they are light brown on all sides and almost cooked through. Leave the insides a bit crunchy. As each batch is done, drain on paper towels, put into a dish, sprinkle with a dash of salt and a crunch of the pepper-grinder, and cover.

Heat 2¹/₂ tsp oil in 3.4 litre (6 pint) heavy-bottomed pot over medium flame. When very hot, stir in the cumin seeds. As soon as they change colour (about 10 seconds), add the rice and stir for 2 to 3 minutes. Pour in 750 ml (1¹/₄ pints) water. Add 1 tsp salt. Stir and bring to the boil. Cover and turn heat very low. Cook for about 25 minutes.

Lift cover off rice pot and quickly (also carefully) lay the flowerets on top of the rice. Cover pot again, and cook for about 10 minutes, until cauliflower is heated through.

To serve: Very carefully move all the cauliflower to one side of the pot. Spoon the rice onto a large platter first, then lay the cauliflower on top of the rice.

Serve with any combination of meats, vegetables and lentils. This again is a very useful and versatile dish that goes well with most English roasts and chops.

Rice with spinach

Serves 6

---

340 g (12 oz) long-grain rice
3 tsp salt
675 g (1½ lb) fresh spinach or a
    340 g (12 oz) package chopped
    frozen spinach

6 tbsp vegetable oil
2 medium-sized onions, peeled and
    finely chopped
1 tsp garam masala

Wash rice thoroughly in colander. Invert into large bowl, and cover with cold water and 1 teaspoon of the salt. Leave for 2 hours.

Fill a 4.5–5.7 litre (8–10 pint) pot with water. Add 1 tsp salt and bring to the boil.

If you are using fresh spinach, trim and wash thoroughly, making sure all the sand is out. Wilt the spinach by dropping it, a little at a time, in the boiling water. As the spinach wilts, remove it to a colander and rinse with cold water. Squeeze the moisture out by pressing between palms of hands, and put on chopping board. When all the spinach is done, chop very finely. (*Or:* following package directions, cook frozen spinach until it is just defrosted. Drain, then squeeze out moisture.)

In a 3.4–4.5 litre (6–8 pint) flameproof and ovenproof casserole, heat the oil, add the onions, and sauté on medium flame for about 5 minutes. They should just turn golden. Now put in the chopped spinach and garam masala. Sauté for about 30 minutes.

Preheat oven to 150°C (300°F) mark 2.

Drain rice and add to spinach with 600 ml (1 pint) water and 1 tsp salt; bring to the boil. Lower heat and simmer for 15 minutes, stirring occasionally.

Cut aluminium foil to cover top of pot snugly. Cut a hole about 1 cm (½ inch) in diameter in the centre of the foil to let the steam escape and the rice dry out. Place foil-covered dish in the middle of the oven for 30 minutes. Check to see if rice is done. If not, leave 5 minutes longer.

Even though this dish is best served straight out of the oven, you can, if necessary, cook it 3 or 4 hours earlier. When cooked, leave it out for 5 minutes with foil on. Then cover it with a tight lid, but do not refrigerate. Fifteen minutes before serving reheat it in a preheated 150°C (300°F) mark 2 oven for 15 minutes.

To serve: Spinach rice can be served plain or garnished with Fried Onion Rings.

Rice with black-eyed peas

Serves 6

---

115 g (4 oz) black-eyed peas (lobhia) soaked overnight in 600 ml (1 pint) water with ½ tsp baking soda 2 tbsp vegetable oil	7 whole cloves 7 black peppercorns 340 g (12 oz) long-grain rice 1 tsp garam masala 1½ tsp salt

---

Empty black-eyed peas and liquid into a pot. Add 300 ml (½ pint) water and ½ tsp salt. Bring to the boil. Skim off all the froth. Cover and simmer gently for 4 to 5 minutes. Drain and discard liquid.

In a 4.5 litre (8 pint) heavy-bottomed pot, heat oil over medium heat. When hot, add cloves and peppercorns and fry until they expand (10 to 20 seconds). Put in the rice and black-eyed peas and fry for 5 minutes. Add the garam masala, 1 tsp salt and 750 ml (1¼ pints) water. Bring to the boil, cover, lower flame to very low, and leave for 30 minutes. Lift cover to see if rice is done. If not, cover and cook for another 5 minutes. Turn flame off. Covered rice will stay warm for 15 to 20 minutes.

To serve: Place on a warm platter, gently breaking lumps with back of large spoon.

For Western meals try serving this with pork or lamb roasts and chops. It is also good with roast duck. Or try it with a German or Polish sausage accompanied with grilled tomatoes and mustard or beetroot greens!

For an Indian meal, have it with Pork Chops Cooked with Whole Spices and Tamarind Juice. Serve some kind of yogurt dish with it.

Rice with yellow split peas

Serves 4

---

115 g (4 oz) yellow split peas	½ tsp whole cumin seeds
4 tsp salt	2-4 small white boiling onions,
170 g (6 oz) long-grain rice	peeled
2 tbsp vegetable oil	3 tbsp butter

Soak split peas in 450 ml (¾ pint) cold water and leave for an hour. Preheat oven to 150°C (300°F) mark 2.

Bring 1.1 litres (2 pints) of water and 1 tsp salt to the boil. When the water is boiling rapidly, drain the split peas and put them in. Boil rapidly for 6 to 7 minutes, and drain.

In a large pot bring 2.8 litres (5 pints) of water and 3 tsp salt to a rolling boil, put in the rice, and boil rapidly for 5 minutes. Drain.

In a 3.4–4.5 litre (6–8 pint) flameproof and ovenproof dish, heat the oil over medium heat. When hot, put in the cumin seeds and fry for 10 to 20 seconds, until they begin to change colour. Add the onions, rolling them around once, then add the drained rice and the drained split peas and fry for 2 to 3 minutes, stirring frequently.

Cut the butter into 3 patties and place on top of rice. Cut a sheet of aluminium foil 5 cm (2 inches) wider than the rim of the dish. Cover dish with it. Place the lid on top. Now crinkle the protruding aluminium around the edges to seal them. Place dish in oven for 45 to 60 minutes. Check after 45 minutes and leave longer only if not yet done.

To serve: Spoon out onto warm platter and serve with any other meat and vegetable combination you like.

Spiced rice with cashew nuts

Serves 6

This dish can be found, with interesting local variations, all over India. It is not hot, just lightly, fragrantly spiced.

---

long-grain rice or Indian basmati rice, measured to the 450 ml (15 fl oz) level in a glass measuring jug
4 tbsp vegetable oil
2 tbsp raw cashew nuts, split in half lengthwise
1 medium-sized onion, peeled, cut in half lengthwise, then sliced into paper-thin half rings

1 clove garlic, peeled and finely chopped
1 tsp peeled, grated fresh ginger
1/2 tsp finely chopped fresh hot green chilli or 1/8 tsp cayenne pepper
3/4 tsp garam masala
1 tsp salt
750 ml (1 1/4 pint) hot vegetable stock or water

Place rice in a bowl. Add water to cover. Rub the rice grains with your hands. Drain the water. Add more water and repeat the process four or five times until the rice is well washed (the water should not be milky). Cover the rice with 1 litre (1 3/4 pints) of fresh water and leave to soak for half an hour. Drain, and leave rice in a strainer.

Preheat oven to 170°C (325°F) mark 3.

This rice dish cooks on top of the stove and in the oven, so it is more convenient to use a heavy, flame- and ovenproof, 2.3 litre (4 pint) sauté pan. Heat the oil over medium heat. Put in the split cashew nuts. Fry for a few seconds, stirring all the time, until they turn a golden brown. Remove with slotted spoon and leave on kitchen paper to drain.

Put the onion slices into the same oil. Fry them for 2 to 3 minutes or until they turn brown at the edges. Add the drained rice, the garlic, ginger, green chilli, garam masala and salt. Turn the heat to medium-low. Stir and fry the rice for 7 to 8 minutes or until the rice is translucent and well coated with the oil.

Add the heated stock. Keep stirring and cooking on a medium-low flame for another 5 to 6 minutes. When the top of the rice begins to look dry (there will still be a little liquid left at the bottom of the pot), cover with a well-fitting lid (or aluminium foil plus a looser-fitting lid) and place in the oven for 20 to 25 minutes or until rice is cooked through. Remove rice pan from the oven and leave, covered, in a warm place for 10 minutes. (If kept covered and in a warm place, this rice will retain its heat for a good half hour.)

Remove rice gently with a slotted spoon, and place on warmed serving platter. Break up all lumps with the back of the slotted spoon. Garnish with the cashew nuts and serve immediately.

Vegetable pullao

Serves 6

---

185 g (6¹/₂ oz) whole mung beans, picked over and washed

long-grain rice, measured to the 450 ml (15 fl oz) level in a glass measuring jug

4¹/₂ tbsp vegetable oil

1 tsp whole black mustard seeds

1 medium-sized onion, peeled and finely chopped

4 medium-sized cloves garlic, peeled and finely chopped

1 tsp peeled, finely chopped fresh ginger

140 g (5 oz) string beans, trimmed and cut into 0.5 cm (¹/₄ inch) long pieces

115 g (4 oz) medium-sized mushrooms, diced into 0.5 cm (¹/₄ inch) pieces

2 tsp garam masala

1¹/₂ tsp ground coriander

2¹/₂ tsp salt

2 tbsp finely chopped fresh green coriander, or parsley

Put mung beans in a bowl with 750 ml (1¹/₄ pints) of water. Cover lightly and set aside for 12 hours. Drain beans and wrap in a very damp tea towel. Put the wrapped bundle in a bowl. Put this bowl in a dark place (like an unused oven) for 24 hours.

Wash rice well and soak in 900 ml (1¹/₂ pints) of water for half an hour. Drain well.

Preheat oven to 170°C (325°F) mark 3.

Heat oil in a wide, heavy, 4.5–5.7 litre (8–10 pint) ovenproof pot over a medium-high flame. When hot, put in the mustard seeds. As soon as the mustard seeds begin to pop (this takes just a few seconds), put in the onion. Stir and fry for about 5 minutes or until onion turns brown at the edges. Add the garlic and ginger. Fry, stirring, for about 1 minute. Turn heat to medium-low and add the mung beans, rice, string beans, mushrooms, garam masala, ground coriander and salt. Stir and sauté for about 10 minutes or until rice turns translucent and vegetables are well coated with oil. Add 900 ml (1½ pints) hot water and the chopped coriander. Turn heat to a medium-high flame and cook, stirring, for about 5 minutes or until most of the water is absorbed. (There will be 2.5 cm (1 inch) or so of water at the bottom.) Cover the pot first with aluminium foil, crimping and sealing the edges, and then with its own lid. Place in heated oven for half an hour. Fluff up with a fork and serve.

Fried onion rings for garnishing

vegetable oil, enough to have at least 2.5 cm (1 inch) in pan

1 medium-sized onion

Heat oil in small frying-pan over medium heat. Peel onion and slice very finely. Wipe onion rings with paper towels and drop into heated fat. As they fry, separate rings with slotted spoon. Fry until rich brown (they should be a rich dark brown without being burned!). Remove with slotted spoon and drain on paper towel. (This can be done ahead of time and the garnish left uncovered in a saucer.) Arrange onion rings over rice or meats.

DALS

Dals – lentils or pulses – are varieties of dried beans and peas. In some form or other they are eaten daily in almost every Indian home, frequently providing the poor with their only source of protein. While people in England and America speak of making their living as earning their 'bread and butter', Indians who earn a bare wage complain that they make just enough for their *'dal roti'* (*roti* is bread).

Both the rice eaters and the wheat eaters of India consume dal with equal enthusiasm. Each state, however, cooks its dals in a completely different way. Punjab excels in whole, unhulled dals – whole *urad* and *rajma* cooked slowly in the clay oven (*tandoor*), as well as in *chana bhatura*, a spicy dish of chickpeas eaten with puffy deep-fried bread. The fussy Delhi-*wallahs* like the hulled and split *moong dal*, delicately spiced with cumin and sprinkled with lime juice and browned onions. In Bombay, a hot, sweet and sour *toovar dal* is made by the addition of tamarind paste and jaggery (a dry, lump variety of molasses) to the cooked dal. In Madras, the scorchingly spicy dal often contains vegetables – aubergines, okra or tomatoes.

In America and England, where a very thin watery dal is often served in Indian and Pakistani restaurants, people have come to the conclusion that dal is a soup. Well, it isn't; a well-cooked dal is generally quick thick. It is hard to describe the exact consistency: it is thinner than porridge, but not quite as thin as pea soup. Having made that generalization, let me add that in some dal recipes the grains stay dry and almost whole, while in others, particularly some cooked in southern India, the dal is indeed quite soupy.

Dal is always eaten with rice or Indian breads. It can be poured over rice, especially when it is thin, or placed beside the rice, or half can be poured over the rice and the rest beside it on the plate. This way it can be eaten with the rice or with other vegetables. It leaves more options open, and is the way I prefer to do it.

What gives dal dishes their final flavour or pep is the *tarka*, or *baghar* or *chhownk*. This does to the dal with a *rouille* does to a fish soup in the south of France. It makes it come alive! You can 'give a *tarka*' of whole mustard seeds or cumin seeds or fenugreek seeds, or of asafetida and cumin seeds, or of browned onions and ginger, and so on. Basically what happens is that oil or ghee is heated in a small pot or frying-pan. Whole spices are added, and the ghee and spices are then poured over the cooked dal.

Here is a list of the commonly used dals; you should learn to recognize them by their shape and colour.

MOONG DAL Hulled and split: small, yellow, rectangular grains; unhulled and whole: small, green, cylindrical grain, called mung beans in health food stores.

URAD DAL Hulled and split: small, off-white rectangular grains; unhulled and whole: small black, cylindrical grain.

CHANA DAL Hulled and split: round, yellow grain, larger than *moong dal*. This dal is of the chickpea family.

ARHAR or *TOOVAR DAL* Hulled and split: round, dull yellow grain, slightly larger than *chana dal* and often with irregular edges.

RAJMA Whole and unhulled: red kidney bean, which comes in a medium and small size.

MASOOR DAL Hulled and split: very tiny, round, shiny salmon-coloured grains that turn yellow when cooked.

KALA CHANA Whole and unhulled: small black chickpeas.

CHHOLA or *KABLI CHANA* Whole: chickpeas or garbanzos.

LOBHIA Whole: black-eyed peas.

Lentils

Serves 6–8

This is a recipe for the dry lentils as bought in an English supermarket.

---

450 g (1 lb) lentils
1 cinnamon stick, 5–7.5 cm
   (2–3 inches) long
1 bay leaf
5 cloves garlic, peeled
2 slices fresh, peeled ginger, 3 mm
   (1/8 inch) thick, and about 2.5 cm
   (1 inch) in diameter
1 tsp ground turmeric

3/4 lemon
11/2 tsp salt
1/8 tsp freshly ground black pepper
1/4–1/2 tsp cayenne pepper (optional)
3 tbsp vegetable oil or ghee
a pinch ground asafetida or tiny
   lump asafetida
1/2 tsp whole cumin seeds

Wash the lentils. Drain.

In a 3.4 litre (6 pint) heavy-bottomed pot, combine the lentils, 1.4 litres (2½ pints) water, cinnamon stick, bay leaf, garlic cloves, ginger slices and turmeric. Bring to the boil. Cover, lower heat, and simmer gently until tender, about 30 to 45 minutes.

Slice lemon into 5 or 6 rounds. Remove seeds. Lift cover of pot and put in the lemon slices, salt, black pepper and cayenne. Stir, cover and simmer for another 5 minutes.

Just before serving, heat the vegetable oil in a 10–15 cm (4–6 inch) frying-pan over medium-high heat. When very hot, put in the asafetida and the cumin seeds. As soon as the asafetida begins to sizzle and expand, and the cumin seeds darken, pour the contents of frying-pan over the lentils and stir.

To serve: Serve the lentils with rice or any of the breads. A meat, chicken, or fish dish and a vegetable would complete the meal.

Chana masaledar

Serves 6

Chickpeas (large *chanas*) are cooked with onion, garlic, ginger, and the *garam* (hot) spices. This is a traditional 'snack' dish from the state of Punjab.

---

170 g (6 oz) chickpeas (large chanas) soaked overnight in 900 ml (1½ pints) water with ¼ tsp baking soda

4-5 tbsp vegetable oil

¼ tsp whole cumin seeds

1 medium-sized onion, peeled and chopped

1–1½ tsp garam masala

1 tsp ground coriander

2 cloves garlic, peeled and minced

a piece of fresh ginger, about 1 cm (½ inch) square, peeled and grated

1 tbsp tomato purée

1½–2 tsp salt

⅛–¼ tsp cayenne pepper

1 tsp ground amchoor or 1 tbsp lemon juice

Garnish

1 firm tomato, washed and quartered

1 medium-sized onion, peeled, halved and cut into coarse slivers

4 fresh hot green chillies (only if someone is going to eat them; otherwise use 4 long slices of a green pepper)

Empty chickpeas and liquid into a large pot. Add 600 ml (1 pint) water, 1 tsp salt and bring to the boil. Remove froth. Cover, lower heat and simmer gently for about 1 hour or until chickpeas are tender. Turn off heat, remove cover and leave chickpeas in liquid.

Heat the oil in a heavy-bottomed 25 cm (10 inch) frying-pan over a medium-high flame. When hot, put in the whole cumin seeds. As soon as they begin to darken, after a few seconds, add the chopped onion. Stir and fry for 7 to 8 minutes or until onion begins to turn a golden brown.

Turn heat to low and add the garam masala and coriander.

Mix, add the garlic and ginger, and fry, stirring for 2-3 minutes. Add the tomato purée and stir again.

Drain the chickpeas, reserving about 150 ml (¼ pint) of the liquid. Pour this into the frying-pan. Add the chickpeas, ½ tsp salt, cayenne and *amchoor* or lemon juice. Mix well, cover, and let the chickpeas cook with the spices for about 30 minutes. Check the salt, adding more if necessary. Stir gently every now and then, taking care not to break the chickpeas.

To serve: Traditionally, the *chanas* (chickpeas) are placed in a bowl lined around the edge with quartered tomatoes, raw onion slivers and green chillies, and then eaten with *bhaturas*. I have served them with *pooris* as well as with rice. A meal with Chicken Moghlai, Prawn Kerala Style, and these chickpeas as well as Cucumber Raita served with plain rice is very nice. This dish can be prepared a day in advance, covered, and refrigerated. Reheat gently over a low flame.

Black-eyed peas (lobhia)

Serves 6

225 g (8 oz) black-eyed peas soaked overnight in 1.1 litres (2 pints) water with 1/4 tsp baking soda
2 tsp salt
3 tbsp vegetable oil
a generous pinch ground asafetida or tiny lump asafetida
1/2 tsp whole cumin seeds
11/2 medium-sized onions, peeled and chopped

1/4 tsp ground turmeric
1 tsp ground coriander
1 tsp ground cumin
1 teacup tomato sauce (see page 114)
1/4–1/2 tsp cayenne pepper (optional)
3 tbsp tamarind paste or 2 tbsp lemon juice

Empty black-eyed peas and liquid into a pot. Add 450 ml (3/4 pint) water and 1 tsp salt. Bring to the boil. Skim off all the froth. Cover and simmer gently for 4 to 5 minutes. Drain and discard the liquid.

In another 3.4 litre (6 pint), heavy-bottomed pot, heat the oil over a medium-high flame. When hot, put in the asafetida and the cumin seeds. As soon as the asafetida expands and sizzles and the cumin seeds darken (this will take a few seconds), put in the chopped onions. Fry onions, stirring, for 7 to 8 minutes, or until they are lightly browned. Add the turmeric, coriander and cumin, and cook, stirring, for 1 minute. Put in the tomato sauce, lower heat, and simmer for 5 minutes, stirring now and then.

Add the black-eyed peas, 150 ml (1/4 pint) water, the rest of the salt (1–11/2 tsp), the cayenne and the tamarind paste. Bring to the boil. Cover, lower heat, and simmer gently for 25 to 35 minutes. Lift off cover, and if there is any extra sauce, turn up heat and boil it down, stirring. All the sauce must adhere to the peas.

To serve: This versatile dish can be served with pork or lamb roasts as well as with almost any Indian meal.

Chick peas with garlic and ginger

Serves 6

---

170 g (6 oz) chickpeas (large chanas) soaked overnight in 900 ml (1½ pints) water with ¼ tsp baking soda

10 cloves garlic, peeled and chopped

a piece of fresh ginger, 5 cm (2 inches) long and 2.5 cm (1 inch) wide, peeled and chopped

5 tbsp vegetable oil

a pinch of ground asafetida or a tiny lump asafetida

½ tsp ground turmeric

3 medium-sized tomatoes (tinned or fresh), peeled and finely chopped

4 medium-sized potatoes, freshly boiled and peeled

2 tsp salt

⅛ tsp freshly ground black pepper

½ tsp cayenne pepper (less if desired)

2 tbsp lemon juice

Empty chickpeas and liquid into a large pot. Add 600 ml (1 pint) water, 1 tsp salt and bring to the boil. Remove froth. Cover, lower heat and simmer gently for 1 hour or until chickpeas are tender. Turn off heat. Drain the chickpeas, reserving 300 ml (½ pint) of the liquid.

Put the garlic, ginger and tomatoes into the container of an electric blender. Add 2 tbsp water and blend until you have a smooth paste.

Heat oil in a large frying-pan or a 25 cm (10 inch) heavy-bottomed pot over a medium flame. When hot, put in the asafetida. After a few seconds, as soon as it sizzles and expands, pour in the paste from the blender, keeping face averted, and add the turmeric. Stir and fry this for 1 to 2 minutes. Now pour in the 300 ml (½ pint) liquid and add the chickpeas. Quarter the potatoes and add them as well. Put in 1 tsp salt, black pepper, cayenne and lemon juice. Bring to the boil, cover, lower heat and simmer gently for 30 minutes.

These chickpeas taste best with some kind of Indian bread – pooris, parathas, or bhaturas. Serve yogurt or cucumber relishes as an accompaniment. Any meat or chicken dish would go with this too.

Moong dal

Serves 6

This is North India's most popular dal, and it is eaten with equal relish by toothless toddlers, husky farmers, and effete urban snobs. The simple recipe given below can be used for the white urad dal, the salmon-coloured masoor dal, and the large arhar or toovar dal as well.

---

285 g (10 oz) moong dal (hulled and split)
2 cloves garlic, peeled
2 slices peeled fresh ginger, 2.5 cm (1 inch) square and 3 mm (1/8 inch) thick
1 tsp chopped fresh green coriander
1 tbsp ground turmeric
1/4–1/2 tsp cayenne pepper (optional)
1 1/2 tsp salt
1 1/2 tbsp lemon juice
3 tbsp vegetable oil or ghee
a pinch ground asafetida or tiny lump asafetida
1 tsp whole cumin seeds
lemon or lime wedges

Clean and wash *dal* thoroughly. Put *dal* in heavy-bottomed 3.4 litre (6 pint) pot, add 1.1 litres (2 pints) water, and bring to the boil. Remove the froth and scum that collects at the top. Now add the garlic, ginger, coriander, turmeric and cayenne pepper. Cover, leaving the lid very slightly ajar, lower heat, and simmer gently for about 1 1/2 hours. Stir occasionally. When *dal* is cooked, add the salt and lemon juice (it should be thicker than pea soup, but thinner than porridge).

In a 10–15 cm (4–6 inch) frying-pan or small pot, heat the vegetable oil or ghee over a medium-high flame. When hot, add the asafetida and cumin seeds. As soon as the asafetida sizzles and expands and the cumin seeds turn dark (this will take only a few seconds), pour the oil and spices over the dal and serve. (Some people put the dal in a serving dish and then pour the oil and spices over it.)

To serve: Serve with plain rice, Kheema, and a vegetable for a simple meal. Most meat and chicken dishes go well with this dal. Since some people like to squeeze extra lemon or lime juice on their dal, serve some wedges separately.

Kala chana aur aloo (black chickpeas with potatoes)

Serves 4

---

170 g (6 oz) black chickpeas (kala
   chana)
1½ tsp salt
½ tsp baking soda
1 medium-sized onion, peeled and
   chopped
3 cloves garlic, peeled and chopped
a piece of fresh ginger about 2.5 cm
   (1 inch) square, peeled and
   chopped
3 tbsp vegetable oil

a generous pinch ground asafetida
   or tiny lump asafetida
¼ tsp whole cumin seeds
4 medium-sized potatoes, peeled
   and quartered
1 tsp ground coriander
¼ tsp ground turmeric
1 tsp garam masala
¼–½ tsp cayenne pepper
3–4 tbsp tamarind paste or 2 tbsp
   lemon juice

Sort and clean the chickpea and wash them under cold water. Drain. Soak for 24 hours in a bowl containing ½ tsp of the salt, the baking soda and 1 litre (1¾ pints) of water.

Place chopped onion, garlic and ginger in the container of an electric blender with 3 tbsp of water. Blend at high speed until you have a smooth paste.

In a 3.4 litre (6 pint) heavy-bottomed pot, heat the oil over a medium-high flame. When very hot, put in the asafetida and the cumin seeds. After a few seconds, when the asafetida expands and the cumin darkens, put in the paste from the blender, keeping face averted. Fry, stirring, for about 5 minutes.

Now drain the chickpeas and add them to the pot. Also put in the potatoes, coriander, turmeric, garam masala, 1 tsp salt, the cayenne pepper and 450 ml (¾ pint) of water. Bring to the boil. Cover, and allow to simmer gently for 1 hour.

Add 3 to 4 tbsp of tamarind paste or lemon juice (you could use more or less) to chickpeas according to tartness desired. Stir. Check salt. Cook for another 10 minutes, stirring occasionally.

To serve: This dish tastes very good with hot pooris or parathas. Some kind of relish – perhaps Cucumber and Tomato with Lemon Juice – should be served with it. For a more complete meal add meat and a green vegetable dish.

Cold chana dal with potatoes

Serves 4

In this dish the *chana dal* is first boiled and then mixed with diced boiled potatoes, salt, pepper, cayenne pepper, roasted cumin and lemon juice. If you like, you can slice spring onions and add them as well. It is served at room temperature or, if you wish, just very slightly chilled.

---

85 g (3 oz) chana dal, cleaned and washed
1 tsp salt
3 peeled slices fresh ginger, about 2.5 cm (1 inch) in diameter and 3 mm (1/8 inch) thick
4 new potatoes, boiled and diced into 1 cm (1/2 inch) cubes

1/8 tsp freshly ground pepper
1 tsp roasted, ground cumin seeds
2 tbsp lemon juice, or 3 tbsp tamarind paste
1/8–1/4 tsp cayenne pepper (optional)

Put the dal to boil with 750 ml (1¼ pints) of water, ½ tsp salt and the ginger slices. Cover, simmer gently for 1 hour. Drain. Discard ginger slices.

In a serving bowl, combine the dal, ½ tsp salt and the remaining ingredients. Mix well.

To serve: Serve with lamb roast or pork chops. Indians often eat this as a snack, at tea-time.

Karhi

Serves 6–8

This dish looks like a very thick soup with dumplings. It is usually eaten with plain rice, and it was a great Sunday favourite with my family. It is made with chickpea flour (*besan*) and buttermilk (the more sour the buttermilk, the better), flavoured with fennel, cumin, fenugreek and mustard seeds.

For the karhi
85 g (3 oz) chickpea flour (besan)
450 ml (³/4 pint) buttermilk
2 tbsp vegetable oil
1 generous pinch ground asafetida
   or tiny lump asafetida
¹/4 tsp whole fennel seeds
¹/4 tsp whole cumin seeds
¹/4 tsp whole black mustard seeds
¹/8 tsp whole fenugreek seeds
¹/4 tsp black onion seeds (kalonji), if
   available

2-3 whole dried hot peppers
1 tsp ground turmeric
1¹/2–2 tsp salt
2-3 tbsp lemon juice

For the pakoris, or dumplings
115 g (4 oz) chickpea flour (besan)
¹/2 tsp baking powder
¹/2 tsp salt
¹/2 tsp ground cumin
vegetable oil for deep frying

To make the karhi: Sift the 85 g (3 oz) chickpea flour into a bowl. Add 150 ml (¹/4 pint) of the buttermilk, a little at a time, and mix well until you have a thick, smooth paste. Now add the remaining 300 ml (¹/2 pint) buttermilk, mixing as you pour it in. Add 1.1 litres (2 pints) of water to the bowl, mix again, and set aside.

In a heavy-bottomed 3.4-4.5 litre (6–8 pint) pot, heat the oil over medium-high flame. When hot, put in the asafetida. In a few seconds, as soon as the asafetida expands, add the fennel, cumin, mustard, fenugreek and onion seeds. When the seeds darken, put in the dry peppers. When they start to darken, add the turmeric, and a second later, the liquid from the bowl. Bring to the boil, cover, lower heat, and simmer gently for 1 hour.

Add salt and lemon juice. Cook another 10 minutes covered. Turn off heat.

To make pakoris, or dumplings (these can be made while *karhi* is cooking): Sift the 115 g (4 oz) of chickpea flour and the baking powder into a bowl. Add salt and cumin. Add water slowly, mixing as you go, until you have a very thick, doughy paste – thick enough to stand in peaks. You will need about 100 ml (4 fl oz) of water, perhaps a little less.

The ideal utensil for deep-frying pakoris is a *karhai* or Chinese wok. If you do not have one, use any other utensil you find convenient. Put at least 6.5 cm (2½ inches) of oil in and heat over a medium-low flame. Give it 10 minutes to heat. Meanwhile, fill a large bowl halfway with warm water and set it somewhere near you.

When the oil is heated, drop the doughy paste, a teaspoonful at a time, into the oil, using a second teaspoon to help release the paste. Make sure you do not drop one dumpling right on top of another. Put in enough to cover the surface and no more. The dumplings will sink first and then rise and float. Fry each batch slowly, for 6 to 7 minutes, turning them at least once; they must not brown. If they begin to darken, lower your flame. They should retain their yellowish colour, but cook through. As soon as each batch is done, lift them out with a slotted spoon and drop into the warm water. Let them soak 2 minutes, then remove from the water and squeeze them very gently, taking care not to break them. Set them aside, covered.

When the karhi is done and the heat turned off, lift the cover and put all the dumplings in. Stir gently. Do not cook the karhi and the dumplings together until 10 minutes before you are ready to eat. Otherwise the dumplings will disintegrate. Now you can bring the karhi to the boil, covered. Lower the heat and simmer gently for 10 minutes.

To serve: Take karhi and pakoris carefully out of the pot so as not to break the pakoris. Place in serving bowl. Serve with plain rice, Khare Masale Ka Gosht, a vegetable and a relish.

Whole unhulled urad and rajma dal

Serves 6

The whole unhulled dals, particularly *urad* and *rajma*, take a very long time to cook. This recipe takes 5 hours. You can, however, take comfort from the fact that they are effortless hours. Once you put the dal on, apart from an occasional stir, not much else is required of you.

---

85 g (3 oz) whole unhulled moong dal, cleaned and washed
85 g (3 oz) whole unhulled rajma dal, cleaned and washed
a piece of fresh ginger, about 1 cm (1/2 inch) cube, peeled and sliced
2 cloves of garlic, peeled
5 tbsp plain yogurt
1/8 tsp cayenne pepper (optional)
13/4 tsp salt
1/8 tsp freshly ground pepper

3 tbsp vegetable oil or ghee
1 medium-sized onion, cut in half lengthwise, then finely sliced
a piece of fresh ginger, about 1 cm (1/2 inch) cube, peeled and grated
a pinch of ground asafetida or a small lump about 3 mm (1/8 inch) square
1/2 tsp whole cumin seeds
2 dried hot red peppers

In a very heavy-bottomed pot, combine the two *dals*, 1.1 litres (2 pints) water, the sliced ginger and the garlic cloves. Bring to the boil, cover, lower heat, and simmer gently for 4 1/2 hours, stirring every hour or so.

Put the yogurt in a small bowl. Beat well with a fork. When the *dal* has cooked for 4 1/2 hours, lift off cover and mash it well against the sides of the pot with the back of a kitchen spoon. Pour in the yogurt, stirring as you do so. Also add the cayenne, salt and pepper. Stir, bring to the boil, cover, lower heat, and simmer for another 30 minutes.

Heat the oil or ghee in an 20–25 cm (8–10 inch) frying-pan. When hot, put in the sliced onion. Fry, stirring, over medium-high flame for about 4 minutes, then put in the grated ginger and fry it along with the onions for 1 more minute, or until onions are brown and crisp. Remove onions and ginger with slotted spoon and set aside.

In the same oil put the asafetida, cumin and red peppers. If the oil is very hot, the cumin and peppers will darken immediately. Turn off heat and pour contents of frying-pan into the pot with the dal. Cover pot again and leave until you are ready to serve.

To serve: Mix the dal and ladle it into warm serving bowl. Sprinkle browned onions and ginger over it. At Delhi's famous Moti Mahal restaurant, a common order with this dal is Tandoori Chicken, naan, and Onions Pickled in Vinegar.

Sambar

Serves 4–6

This South Indian dal may be cooked in combination with almost any vegetable. Carrots, long beans (found in Chinese and Indian grocery stores), ordinary green beans, aubergine, marrow and cauliflower should be sliced or diced and then lightly steamed before being added to the cooked dal. Vegetables like okra, onions, radish (white or red) and kohlrabi should be sliced and lightly sautéed in oil or ghee before being mixed in with the cooked dal.

Traditionally, sambar is made very, very hot with fistfuls of dried hot red peppers. I have used ground cayenne pepper, which you can adjust to your own taste. Also, in South India, this dal is cooked with enough water to make it thin and soup-like. It is served in individual bowls and eaten with boiled or steamed rice.

125 g (4½ oz) toovar (arhar) dal
2½ tbsp ghee or vegetable oil
a generous pinch of ground asafetida
1 tbsp whole coriander seeds
1½ tsp whole cumin seeds
2-3 tbsp freshly grated coconut, roasted
½ tsp whole black mustard seeds
1 medium-sized onion, halved and thickly sliced
6 radishes, trimmed and thickly sliced
1 medium-sized tomato, peeled and diced
1 tsp whole fenugreek seeds

2 whole cloves
10–12 black peppercorns
a 2 cm (¾ inch) piece of stick cinnamon
¼–½ tsp cayenne pepper
½ tsp ground turmeric
1–2 tbsp tamarind paste
¾–1 tsp salt
¼ tsp sugar
1 fresh hot green chilli, finely chopped
1 tsp finely grated fresh ginger
2 tbsp finely chopped fresh green coriander

Clean and wash the dal. Drain. Add 900 ml (1½ pints) water and bring to the boil. Turn heat to low, cover in such a way as to leave the lid slightly ajar, and simmer gently until the dal is quite tender, about 1½ hours. Stir every now and then during the last 10 minutes of the cooking.

Heat 1 tbsp of the ghee in a small, heavy frying-pan or a very small pot over a medium flame. When hot, put in the asafetida and, a few seconds later, the coriander seeds, cumin, fenugreek, cloves, peppercorns and cinnamon. As soon as the spices turn a few shades darker (this takes just a few seconds), put in the cayenne pepper. Stir once and remove from heat.

Put contents of small frying-pan immediately into the container of an electric blender. Add the roasted, grated coconut and 50 ml (2 fl oz) water. Blend until you have a smooth paste. Set aside.

In a 2.3–3.4 litre (4–6 pint) pot, heat the remaining 1½ tbsp of ghee over a medium flame. When hot, put in the mustard seeds. As soon as the seeds begin to pop (this just takes a few seconds), lower the heat and put in the sliced onion and sliced radishes. Sauté for 3 to 4 minutes. Do not allow any browning. Now add the paste from the blender and stir for a few seconds. Put in the cooked *dal*, the diced tomato, turmeric, the tamarind paste (put in 1 tbsp of the paste first, adding more later if you think you want it), salt and sugar. Add more water, if necessary, to get a thin, soup-like consistency. Stir well, check for seasoning, and bring to the boil. Cover partially, lower heat, and simmer gently for about 10 minutes.

Add the green chilli, ginger and fresh coriander. Simmer, uncovered, for another 2 minutes.

EGGS, YOGURT AND PANEER

Eggs have more usable protein than almost any other food on earth, and, as a double blessing for us, there are such wonderful ways of cooking them. There are lots of delicious ways of turning this simple food into a sustaining and flavourful meal. Tiny amounts of seasoning can make an egg taste entirely different – and very good. Instead of making the more common type of European omelette, try adding handfuls of fresh herbs, such as coriander, or cooked courgettes and cauliflower. Spicy tomatoes are a delicious addition to scrambled eggs. If you are looking for a filling main course for dinner, try the Hard-boiled Eggs in a Spicy Almond Sauce. It is rich, hot, nutty and quite excellent when served with an Indian or Persian pilaf.

Dairy products give nutritional balances to most vegetarian meals, as well as complementing a non-vegetarian diet. Yogurt is eaten in so many different ways in India. When beaten together with grated cucumber and mint, it becomes a *raita;* when added to sautéed courgette, it becomes a delicious accompaniment for rice. It is a protein-rich, easy-to-digest, tasty, versatile food that may be eaten plain or used in soups, cold drinks, breads, sauces, relishes and all manner of main dishes. Paneer is a fresh cheese that is made with curdled milk. Actually, paneer simply means cheese in most North Indian languages but because this particular cheese is popular and well known, it seems to have appropriated the name for itself. A fresh paneer is readily available in Indian bazaars and grocery stores (just as bean curd is in China and Japan), it is seldom made at home. However, making it is not too complicated, though it does require an overnight wait.

Khitcherie unda (scrambled eggs, Indian style)

Serves 2–3

---

3 tbsp butter
1/2 medium-sized onion, finely
   chopped
1 small tomato, chopped
1 tbsp chopped fresh green
   coriander

1/2–1 hot green chilli, finely sliced
4 medium-large eggs, well beaten
salt and pepper to taste

Melt the butter in a 25 cm (10 inch) frying-pan over medium heat. Add onions and sauté them for a minute or until they begin to turn translucent.

Add diced tomato, green coriander and sliced green chilli. Stir and cook for 3 to 4 minutes or until tomatoes soften a bit.

Pour in the beaten eggs. Sprinkle on salt and pepper lightly. Stir and move eggs around with a fork. Indians like their scrambled eggs rather hard (cooked about 3 minutes), but you can stop whenever the desired consistency has been achieved.

To serve: While some Indians eat their scrambled eggs with toast, others eat them with hot parathas, chapatis, or pooris.

Scrambled eggs with spicy tomatoes

Serves 4

I like to make this dish very hot (chilli hot) but you could leave out the green chillies and still have a very tasty dish. Also, if you have no access to good tomatoes, use tinned ones. Just drain them well before chopping them. You should end up with enough drained, chopped tomatoes to fill a 750 ml (1¼ pint) jar.

The thick sauce is nice to have around in the refrigerator or freezer. It serves as an excellent relish and turns into a superb sauce for pasta.

---

450 g (1 lb) ripe tomatoes, peeled
3 tbsp vegetable oil
1½ tsp whole black mustard seeds
60 g (2 oz) very finely sliced spring onions (about 4 whole spring onions, including green)
2 large cloves garlic, peeled and finely chopped (about 1 tbsp)
½ tsp finely grated fresh ginger

3 tbsp finely chopped fresh green coriander
1 fresh hot green chilli (or to taste), finely chopped
½–¼ tsp salt
1⁄16 tsp freshly ground black pepper
7 large eggs
salt to taste

Chop the tomatoes very finely.

Heat the oil in a 20 cm (8 inch) very well-seasoned or nonstick frying-pan over a medium-low flame. When hot, put in the mustard seeds. As soon as the mustard seeds begin to pop (this takes just a few seconds), put in the sliced spring onions and garlic. Stir and fry for about 3 minutes or until the spring onion whites are almost translucent but not browned at all. Now add the tomato pulp, the ginger, fresh coriander and the green chilli. Stir and fry over medium heat for 6 to 8 minutes. The tomatoes should not remain watery. Add ½ tsp salt and the black pepper. Mix, and correct seasonings. Turn off heat.

Beat the eggs lightly with a fork or a whisk. Add less than ¼ tsp salt to the eggs and mix.

Bring the sauce in the frying-pan to a simmer. Turn heat to low. Add the eggs to the pan. Stir gently but continuously to scramble the eggs. Remove from the fire when the right degree of doneness has been achieved. Serve immediately.

Eggs, potatoes and cauliflower

Serves 4–6

This dish can be made ahead of time and reheated.

---

450 g (1 lb) cauliflower (½ small head)

115 g (4 oz) freshly grated coconut

2½ tsp salt

2 smallish tomatoes, 115 g (4 oz), peeled

a 2.5 cm (1 inch) cube of fresh ginger, peeled and cut into 3 or 4 pieces

6-7 cloves garlic, peeled

4 tbsp vegetable oil

½ tsp whole fenugreek seeds

a 2.5 cm (1 inch) stick of cinnamon

1 medium-sized onion, peeled and finely chopped

1-2 fresh hot green chillies, finely chopped

½ tsp ground turmeric

5–6 fresh curry leaves, if available, or 10 dried ones

2 medium-sized potatoes, boiled, cooled, peeled, and cut in half crosswise

2 tbsp lemon juice

½ tsp garam masala

Break cauliflower into flowerets 4 cm (1½ inch) long and 2 cm (¾ inch) at the top.

Put the coconut into the container of a food processor or blender and turn the machine on. Slowly add 250 ml (8 fl oz) hot water. Let the machine run for 1 minute. Strain this mixture through a double thickness of cheesecloth, squeezing out as much liquid as you can. This is the first coconut milk. Set it aside.

Put the coconut that remains in the cheesecloth back into the processor or blender and repeat the process with another 250 ml (8 fl oz) of hot water. After this coconut milk has been strained, set it aside separately from the first. This is the second coconut milk.

Bring about 4.5 litres (8 pints) of water to a rolling boil in a large pot. Add 1 tsp salt to the water. Drop in the cauliflower. Let the water return to the boil and then boil rapidly for 30 seconds. Drain the cauliflower and rinse it immediately under cold running water.

Dice the tomatoes into 0.5 cm (¼ inch) pieces.

Put the ginger, garlic and 50 ml (2 fl oz) water into the container of a blender or food processor and blend until you have a paste.

Heat the oil in a 23–25 cm (9–10 inch) sauté or frying-pan over a medium flame. When hot, first put in the fenugreek seeds and, a couple of seconds later, the cinnamon stick. Now put in the onion. Stir and fry on medium heat for about 2 minutes. Add the ginger-garlic paste and the finely chopped chilli. Stir and fry for another minute. Add the tomatoes, turmeric and curry leaves. Keep stirring and frying for 2 minutes. Now add half of the second coconut milk, cover, turn heat to low and simmer for 10 minutes.

Uncover, add the potatoes, cauliflower, 1½ tsp salt and the remaining half of the second coconut milk. Stir gently to mix and bring to a simmer. Cover, and simmer on low heat for 5 minutes, stirring once or twice during this period. Uncover again and put in the halved eggs, cut side up, the first coconut milk and the lemon juice. Mix very gently, spooning the sauce over the eggs. Cover and simmer another 5 minutes. Sprinkle in the garam masala. Mix gently.

Eggs pulusu

Serves 4 with other dishes

Here is a simple, exceedingly pleasant dish from South India that may be eaten with rice or, as one of my daughters seems to prefer, on slices of toasted bread.

---

1 tsp ground cumin seeds	1 medium-sized onion, peeled and
1 tsp ground coriander seeds	finely chopped
½ tsp ground turmeric	2 tbsp tamarind paste
¼ tsp cayenne pepper	1 tsp salt
3 tbsp vegetable oil	4 large hard-boiled eggs, peeled
	and cut in half crosswise

Mix together the cumin, coriander, turmeric and cayenne in a small cup.

Over a medium-low flame, heat the oil in a sauté or frying-pan that is about 18–20 cm (7–8 inch) wide. Put in the onion. Sauté, stirring, for about 5 minutes. Put in the spice mixture and sauté for another minute. Now put in the tamarind paste, 250 ml (8 fl oz) water and the salt. Cover and simmer on low heat for 2 to 3 minutes. Put in the eggs, cut side up, and spoon some of the sauce over them. Cook the eggs gently for 3 to 4 minutes, spooning the sauce over them again and again.

Hard-boiled eggs in a spicy almond sauce

Serves 4

You may eat this dish with rice or with any bread. I often have it for lunch or dinner with thick slices of French bread and a green salad.

---

30 g (1 oz) blanched, slivered almonds

2 tsp whole cumin seeds

2 tbsp white poppy seeds

1 tsp ground coriander seeds

1 whole dried hot red pepper

5 tbsp vegetable oil

3 whole cardamom pods

1 medium-sized onion, peeled and finely chopped

4 cloves garlic, peeled and finely chopped

a 2 cm (3/4 inch) cube of fresh ginger, peeled and finely chopped

50 ml (2 fl oz) plain yogurt

50 ml (2 fl oz) Spicy Tomato Sauce, (see page 114) or 1 tbsp tomato purée mixed with 3 tbsp water

1 tsp salt, or to taste

100 ml (4 fl oz) single cream

1 tbsp lemon juice

1/2 tsp garam masala

4 hard-boiled eggs, peeled and cut in half crosswise

Put the almonds in a small, heavy frying-pan (cast iron would be best) and stir them around over medium-low heat until they are lightly browned. Then put them into the container of a clean coffee grinder and pulverize them. Remove from coffee grinder.

Put 1 tsp of the cumin seeds, the poppy seeds, coriander seeds and red pepper into the same frying-pan. Stir and dry-roast over medium-low heat until the poppy seeds are a few shades darker (they turn greyish) and a pleasant 'roasted' aroma arises from the frying-pan. This takes just a few minutes. Put these spices in the coffee grinder and pulverize. Leave in coffee grinder.

Heat the oil in a 18–20 cm (7–8 inch) sauté or frying pan over a medium flame. When hot put in the remaining 1 tsp cumin seeds and the whole cardamom pods. Stir and fry for a few seconds until the cardamoms turn a darker shade. Put in the finely chopped onion, garlic and ginger. Stir and fry for about 5 minutes or until the onion mixture is lightly browned. Now put in 1 tbsp of the yogurt. Stir and cook for about 30 seconds or until the yogurt is incorporated into the onion mixture. Add the remaining yogurt 1 tbsp at a time in exactly the same way. Now put in the tomato sauce, also 1 tbsp at a time, incorporating it into the sauce each time just as you did the yogurt. Put in the ground spices sitting in the coffee grinder and stir for 10 seconds. Put in the ground almonds and stir for another 10 seconds. Add 250 ml (8 fl oz) water and the salt. Bring to a simmer. Cover, turn heat to very low and simmer gently for 5 minutes.

Add the cream, lemon juice and garam masala. Stir to mix. Simmer, uncovered, on very low heat for 4 to 5 minutes. Put the eggs into the sauce, cut side up, laying them out in a single layer. Spoon some sauce over them. Simmer the eggs very gently for 7 to 8 minutes, spooning the sauce over them frequently as you do so. Spoon off any oil that rises to the top.

Yogurt with chick peas and tomatoes

Serves 4–6

---

180 g (6 oz) drained, tinned chick peas
a 2.5 cm (1 inch) long cinnamon stick
8 whole cloves
1 tsp whole black peppercorns
1 bay leaf
1 tsp whole cumin seeds
1 tsp whole fennel seeds
1 tsp salt

350 ml (12 fl oz) plain yogurt
2 smallish tomatoes (about 115 g / 4 oz), peeled, and cut into 0.5 cm (1/4 inch) dice
1/2 tsp ground roasted cumin seeds
1/8 tsp freshly ground black pepper
1/8–1/4 tsp cayenne pepper (optional)
1 tbsp finely chopped fresh green coriander (optional)

Put the chick peas in a strainer under running water and wash them well. Leave to drain in the strainer.

Tie the cinnamon, cloves, peppercorns, bay leaf, cumin and fennel seeds in a cheesecloth bundle. Bring 750 ml (1 1/4 pints) of water to the boil. Put in the cheesecloth bundle as well as 1/2 tsp of the salt. Cover, lower heat, and simmer for 15 minutes.

Put the chick peas into the simmering liquid and bring to the boil. Cover, lower heat, and simmer for 5 minutes. Uncover and let the chick peas cool in the liquid. Drain.

In a bowl, combine the yogurt, chick peas, tomatoes, the remaining 1/2 tsp salt, the cumin, black pepper, cayenne and fresh coriander. Mix. Cover and refrigerate until ready to eat.

Yogurt with courgettes

Serves 4–6

This is an absolutely wonderful dish that may be served warm or cold.
I find that I can eat it by the spoonful, all by itself. I often do!

---

2 medium-sized courgettes, about 340-400 g (12–14 oz)	3 tbsp vegetable oil
3/4 tsp salt	1 tsp whole black mustard seeds
1 medium-sized onion	1/16 tsp freshly ground black pepper
350 ml (12 fl oz) plain yogurt	1/16 tsp cayenne pepper (use as much as you like)

Trim the courgettes and grate them coarsely. Put them in a bowl and sprinkle with 1/2 tsp salt. Toss to mix and set aside for half an hour. Drain the courgette and press out as much liquid as you can. Separate the shreds so you do not have lumps.

Peel the onion, cut it in half lengthwise, and then cut into fine, half-moon-shaped slices.

Put the yogurt in a bowl. Beat it lightly with a fork or whisk until it is smooth and creamy.

Heat the oil in a 20 cm (8 inch) frying-pan over a medium flame. When hot, put in the mustard seeds. As soon as the mustard seeds begin to pop (this takes just a few seconds), put in the onion. Stir and fry it for about 2 minutes or until the slices are translucent. Add the courgette. Stir and fry for another 3 minutes. Turn off the heat and let the courgette cool slightly. When cooled, fold it into the yogurt. Add the remaining 1/4 tsp salt, pepper and cayenne. If you wish to eat the dish cold, cover and refrigerate it. If you wish to eat it warm, put the yogurt-courgette combination in a double boiler over a low flame. Then heat, stirring in one direction, until warm. Do not let it boil.

Yogurt with spinach

Serves 4–6

285–450 g (10–16 oz) fresh spinach	1/8–1/4 tsp cayenne pepper (optional)
2 tsp salt	1 tsp freshly roasted, ground cumin seeds
425 g (15 oz) plain yogurt	
1/8–1/4 tsp freshly ground black pepper	

Wash and trim the spinach. Make sure no sand is left. Bring 3.4 litres (6 pints) of water to boil in large pot. Add 1 tsp salt. When boiling, drop spinach in it and cover. As soon as the spinach wilts, remove it and put it in a colander. Run cold water over it until it cools. Drain. Squeeze out the water by pressing spinach between your palms and then mince.

Place the yogurt in a bowl and mix well with a fork. Add the minced spinach, 1 tsp salt, black pepper, cayenne and cumin. Mix well. Cover and refrigerate until ready to serve.

To serve: Serve cold with Lamb Cooked in Dark Almond Sauce or Koftas. Serve also with cauliflower or carrots or potatoes.

Soft yogurt cheese with fresh coriander and spring onions, Gujarati style

Makes enough to fill a 250 ml (8 fl oz) cup

This Gujarati dish is generally served at breakfast and eaten with *khakra*, a fine crispbread, any sprouted mung-bean dish, and a fresh green chutney. Because khakra is a fairly complicated bread to master I have not included a recipe, but you could substitute Scandinavian crispbreads as they are similar to khakras. I often put this cheese out in a 300 ml (1/2 pint) ceramic bowl, filling it all the way to the top and then either smoothing the top or making a design in it with the flat side of a knife, as one would with rough icing. This cheese may be served as a spread with biscuits and crispbreads.

Make sure that the fresh coriander is thoroughly dry before you chop it.

---

450 g (1 lb) whole-milk yogurt
2 tbsp finely chopped fresh green
  coriander

1 tsp finely chopped white part of
  spring onion
1/4 tsp salt
1/2 tsp sugar

Balance a strainer over a bowl. Line the strainer with a tripled thickness of cheesecloth, about 35 cm (14 inch) square. Put the yogurt in the middle of the cheesecloth. Bring the four corners of the cheesecloth together. Now tie the yogurt so as to make a loose bundle. You can do this by using one of four corners of the cheesecloth or by using a piece of string. Alternatively, you could sew a cheesecloth bag, put the yogurt inside the bag, and then tie the bag. Suspend the bundle or bag of yogurt where it can drip. I tie mine to the tap of the kitchen sink. Let it drip for 4 to 5 hours. Remove cheesecloth and combine the yogurt cheese with the other ingredients in a stainless steel or non-metallic bowl. Mix well. Cover and refrigerate for at least 1 hour. If some liquid accumulates, just discard it before you serve.

Shrikhand (sweet soft yogurt cheese with saffron)

Makes enough to fill a 250 ml (8 fl oz) cup and serves 2

This Gujarati cheese, made by hanging yogurt up for just 3 hours, has the consistency of a very, very thick cream. The use of saffron and pistachios makes it somewhat expensive, hence it is generally reserved for weddings and banquets.

You may serve this cheese with a meal or after it. If you serve it as dessert, you may wish to make it even sweeter.

This recipe may be doubled easily by doubling all the ingredients. The time for hanging up the yogurt will, of course, remain the same.

---

450 g (1 lb) plain yogurt, preferably made from whole milk
1/4 tsp leaf saffron
2 tsp warm milk

60 g (2 oz) caster sugar, or less, according to taste
1/8 tsp cardamom seeds
1 tsp shelled, unsalted pistachio nuts, cut into slivers

Follow the directions for making soft yogurt cheese from the previous recipe, without adding the coriander and spring onion. Hang the yogurt up for just 3 hours.

Meanwhile, soak the saffron in the milk for about 1 hour.

Combine the yogurt cheese, saffron milk and sugar in a bowl. Mix well with a fork or whisk until creamy. Push this mixture through a very fine sieve to make sure that there are no lumps left. Crush the cardamom seeds to a powder in a mortar and add them to the yogurt. Spoon this mixture neatly into two small bowls. Sprinkle the pistachios over the top. Cover tautly with cling film and chill until ready to eat.

Paneer (fresh cheese)

This amount, when mixed with vegetables, will serve 6

1.1 litres (2 pints) whole milk   **2½ tbsp lemon juice**

Bring the milk to the boil. As soon as it begins to bubble, put in the lemon juice, stir once, and take the pot off the heat. Leave it for 15 minutes. The milk will curdle and the curds will separate from the whey.

Strain the curds through 3 layers of cheesecloth. Squeeze out as much whey as you can easily. (Do not discard this whey. Refrigerate it and use it in cooking instead of water.) Tie up the curds in the cheesecloth, using twine to make a small, round bundle. Use sufficient twine, as you now need to hang up this bundle somewhere to drip overnight. (I just hang it on the tap in the sink.)

Next morning, remove the hanging bundle and untie it. Gently flatten it out to make a 10 cm (4 inch) patty, keeping the cheese loosely wrapped in the cheesecloth. Put the cheesecloth-wrapped cheese patty on a sturdy plate and place a very heavy object 2.3–2.7 kg (5–6 lb) on top of it. I use one of my very heavy, porcelain-covered cast-iron pots filled with water. If the pot seems in danger of tipping over to one side, I balance it by standing appropriately sized jars under its two handles. Leave the weight on the cheese for 4 to 5 hours. After the cheese has been pressed, it should be 1–2 cm (½–¾ inch) thick.

Remove the cheese from the cheesecloth and, with a sharp knife, cut it into cubes, diamond shapes, or rectangles. If your cheese has pressed down to 1 cm (½ inch), diamonds or rectangles no longer than 2.5 cm (1 inch) are best. If the cheese is about 2 cm (¾ inch) thick, it can be cubed.

Note: Some people like to add a little freshly ground pepper and some finely chopped fresh green coriander – 1 tbsp – to the curds just after the whey had been strained, before it is tied and hung up.

Paneer, once made, is quite crumbly and breakable. Because of this, it is generally fried and lightly browned before it is cooked. It is a good idea to do this frying in a well-seasoned cast-iron or Teflon-lined frying pan, as the cheese tends to stick a bit. There are some dishes in which the cheese is not fried at all.

Rather like bean curd, fresh paneer has very little taste of its own. It does have texture – and lots of protein. The taste comes from the flavours of the foods with which it is cooked. In a very traditional dish from the Punjab, paneer is combined with peas and tomatoes. It is frequently cooked with puréed spinach. It can also be crumbled and added to various grated vegetables (like marrow and courgettes) to form 'meatballs'. It can be crumbled, layered with partially cooked rice, and baked.

Matar paneer (peas with paneer)

Serves 6

This Punjabi dish, with some variation in the spices, is eaten over all of North India. Indian restaurants, whether in India or outside it, almost always serve it on their thali, or vegetarian platter.

---

1 medium-sized onion, peeled and chopped

about a 2.5 cm (1 inch) cube fresh ginger, peeled and chopped

6 tbsp vegetable oil

paneer, see page 153 (plus 500 ml (16 fl oz) of the whey)

1 whole dried hot red pepper

1 tbsp ground coriander seeds

1/4 tsp ground turmeric

3 medium-sized tomatoes, peeled and finely chopped

1 tsp salt

1/8 tsp freshly ground black pepper

600 g (11/4 lb) shelled fresh, or 2 packets defrosted frozen, peas

---

Put the chopped onion and ginger into the container of an electric blender or food processor along with 75 ml (3 fl oz) water and blend until you have a smooth paste. Leave paste in the blender container.

Heat the oil in a heavy, 25 cm (10 inch) wide pot (preferably Teflon-lined) over a medium flame. When hot, put in the pieces of paneer in a single layer and fry them until they are a golden brown on all sides. This happens pretty fast. With a slotted spoon remove fried paneer to a plate. Put the dried red pepper into the same oil. Within 2 seconds, turn the pepper over so that it browns on both sides. Now put in the contents of the blender (keep your face averted as the paste might splatter). Fry, stirring constantly, for about 10 to 12 minutes, or until paste turns a light-brown colour.

Add the coriander and turmeric and fry, stirring, for another minute. Put in the chopped tomatoes. Stir and fry for another 3 to 4 minutes or until tomatoes turn a dark, reddish-brown shade. Now pour in 500 ml (16 fl oz) of the whey. Add the salt and the black pepper. Mix well and bring to the boil. Cover, lower heat, and simmer gently for 10 minutes. Lift cover and put in the paneer pieces and the peas. Cover and simmer for 10 minutes or until peas are cooked.

Saag paneer (spinach with paneer)

Serves 4–6

Saag paneer, a combination of greens and paneer, is eaten all over North India with slight variations in the spices. In India, the spinach, which turns into a sauce for the paneer, is sometimes creamed. At other times it is left in its chopped state, thus allowing it to stand in equal partnership with the paneer. I like the latter method because this way the spinach retains its texture.

I use a 30 cm (12 inch) wide, 10 cm (4 inch) high, nonstick sauté pan to make this dish. If you do not have such a pan, fry the paneer separately, in a Teflon or a well-seasoned cast-iron frying-pan. Then transfer the oil to a pot large enough to hold the raw spinach, and continue the cooking.

For this recipe, I have used fresh spinach because I prefer its taste. You could use two packets of frozen, chopped spinach if you like. Cook spinach according to packet directions, drain well, and proceed with the recipe. Do not salt the spinach twice and remember to cook it very briefly with the ginger-garlic mixture.

---

a 2.5 cm (1 inch) cube of fresh ginger, peeled and coarsely chopped
3–6 cloves garlic, peeled
1/2–1 fresh hot green chilli, sliced roughly
paneer (see page 153)
salt

1/4 tsp garam masala
1/4 tsp cayenne pepper (optional)
6 tbsp vegetable oil
675 g (11/2 lb) spinach, washed, trimmed, and very finely chopped
3 tbsp single cream

Put the ginger, garlic and green chilli into the container of an electric blender or food processor along with 50 ml (2 fl oz) water. Blend until you have a smooth paste. You may need to push down with a rubber spatula once.

Heat the oil in a large, wide, preferably nonstick sauté pan over a medium flame. Put in all the pieces of paneer and fry them, turning them over gently with a slotted spatula, until they are golden brown on all sides. (This happens fairly quickly.) Remove paneer with a slotted spoon and place on a plate in a single layer. Sprinkle paneer quickly with the 1/8 tsp salt, the garam masala and the cayenne pepper. Set aside.

Put the paste from the blender into the hot oil in your pan (keep face averted) and fry it, stirring constantly, for about 30 seconds. Now put in the spinach and 1/2 tsp salt. Stir the spinach around for 1 minute. Cover the pan, lower the heat, and let the spinach cook gently with the ginger-garlic paste for 15 minutes. There should be enough water clinging to the spinach leaves to cook them. If all the water evaporates, add 1–2 tbsp and continue cooking.

Now put in the paneer and cream, stir gently, and bring to a simmer. Cover, and continue cooking on low heat for another 10 minutes. Stir once or twice during this period.

BREADS

In India, we call our Indian bread *roti* and we call the Western-type loaf a *dubbul* (double) *roti*, probably because of the expansion caused by the yeast. Most of our everyday breads are unleavened – somewhat like the Mexican tortilla, but much more varied in shape, taste and texture. They are generally made out of whole-wheat flour, though barley, maize, millet, chickpea and plain white flour are also used. We do make leavened breads like the naan, but they tend to be flat, rising only 1 to 2 cm (1/2 to 3/4 inches) in height.

Throughout most of North India *ata*, or finely ground whole-wheat flour, is measured out onto a very large brass platter, or *paraat*, for kneading. This *paraat* is essential because Indian kitchens do not have Formica countertops and because Indians prefer to do most of their kitchen work – chopping, cutting, grinding and kneading – in a squatting position. Once the dough has been kneaded (this is done with clenched fists – the knuckles pressing into the dough), it is formed into a lump, covered with a damp cloth, and left on one side of the *paraat*. Just before cooking, it is kneaded again and made into little patties. These are then rolled out on a round board into chapatis, parathas, or pooris.

Breads are cooked on the *tava*, a heavy, cast-iron, slightly curved plate, or in a *karhai*, a wok-like utensil for deep frying, or they are baked in the clay oven known as the *tandoor*. For a *tava* you can substitute a 20–25 cm (8–10 inch) cast-iron frying-pan; for a *karhai* you can use any wide, heavy casserole-type pot (cast-iron would be excellent); and for the *tandoor*, one just has to use the oven or a charcoal grill.

While Indian rice can be eaten with a fork, Indian bread *must* be eaten with the hands – or rather, with one hand. A small piece of the bread is broken off, wrapped around a morsel of food, and eaten. Only one hand is used – and just the fingertips at that. The other hand has to be kept clean to pass food or pick up a glass of water.

Here are some of the basic breads.

Chapati

Serves 4

This simple bread requires only whole-wheat flour and water. It needs to be rolled out very evenly on a floured surface. Indians keep a quantity of plain whole-wheat flour on the side and keep dusting the chapati with it as they roll. Next, the chapati needs to be cooked on a *tava*. Give the *tava* time to heat before you put the first chapati on. When both sides of the chapati are roasted, it is taken off the *tava* and placed on an open fire. This makes it puff up with hot air. A *chimta* or some flat unserrated tongs are essential for the making of the bread.

115 g (4 oz) finely ground whole-wheat flour for dough	about 55 g (2 oz) finely ground whole-wheat flour to keep on the side for dusting

Place the flour in a bowl. Slowly add up to 100 ml (4 fl oz) water and mix until all the flour adheres and you can knead it. (You will probably need a little less than the 100 ml (4 fl oz) water.) Now knead it for 7 to 8 minutes. Roll into a ball. Cover with a damp cloth and leave for 1/2 to 3 hours. (If you wish to leave it longer, cover it with a plastic wrap and refrigerate. It will easily stay 24 hours.)

Dampen hands and knead the dough again. Put the *tava* or cast-iron frying-pan on a *medium* flame to heat. Knead dough while the *tava* is heating. Divide the dough into 8 balls. Keep balls covered with damp cloth. Flour the rolling surface and keep some dry flour on the side for dusting. Take out one ball. Flatten it. Dip it in the dry flour. Now roll it out evenly into a chapati about 12 cm (5 inches) in diameter. You can get it even bigger and thinner if you like. It will stick to the surface as you roll it unless you keep dipping it in the dry flour. Always keep your surface well floured.

The *tava* or frying-pan should be smoking hot by now. Place the uncooked chapati on it. Within half a minute or so bubbles will start rising. Now turn the chapati over with the *chimta* or tongs. Let the other side cook for half a minute. Both sides should have light brown spots on them. Lift off chapati with the tongs and lay it directly over the medium flame or another burner. (You could use the same burner, but you would have to lift off the *tava* or frying-pan every time. As a matter of fact, this *is* what most Indians do!) Keep it there a few seconds. It will puff up immediately. Now turn it over and keep the other side over the flame for a few seconds.

Either serve hot immediately, or butter on one side very lightly and place chapati on a large sheet of aluminium foil. Fold over the aluminium foil and shut edges firmly. Do all chapatis this way. They will stay warm for 20 to 30 minutes if stacked tightly and kept well covered in foil in a warm place.

Poori

Serves 4–6

The dough here is rather like that of the chapati, only a little oil is added. Some people like to add a bit of salt as well to the dough. It is then kneaded and rolled out. Deep fat is heated in a wok, *karhai*, or deep frying-pan, and the pooris are fried quickly in it. They puff up like the chapati. Pooris can be made ahead of time and wrapped lightly in aluminium foil. They do not stay puffed this way, but they still taste good. They can be reheated (in the foil) in a 150°C (300°F) mark 2 oven for 10 minutes.

---

55 g (2 oz) finely ground whole-
    wheat flour
55 g (2 oz) all-purpose white flour
1½ tbsp vegetable oil
oil for deep frying, enough to have
    5–7.5 cm (2–3 inches) in frying-pan

about 55 g (2 oz) finely ground
    whole-wheat flour to keep on
    the side for dusting

Place whole-wheat and white flour in a bowl. Pour the oil over it. Slowly add up to 100 ml (4 fl oz) water and mix until all the flour adheres and you can knead it. (You will probably need a little less than this amount.) Knead it well for 7 to 8 minutes. Form into a ball, cover with a damp cloth, and leave for 1½ to 3 hours. (If you wish to leave it longer, cover with aluminium foil and refrigerate. It will keep up to 24 hours.)

Heat the oil in the karhai, wok or frying-pan over a medium flame. Give it time to get smoking hot. I wait 10 minutes before I put the first poori in.

While the oil is heating, knead the dough again. Divide the dough into 14 balls, keeping those you are not rolling covered with damp cloth. Flatten the balls one at a time and roll them out this way: first dip the flattened ball in the whole-wheat flour that you have on the side. Now roll it evenly, sprinkling the surface and the poori with flour when you need to, until it is about 9–10 cm (3½–4 inches) in diameter. Do not allow it to stick to the surface. Whenever it does, dip it in the dry flour.

Test the hot oil by dropping a poori in it. It will first sink to the bottom. Then, within a few seconds, it will rise and sizzle. Now you can do one of two things. Either keep pushing the poori down gently – with swift but soft pushes, using the back of a slotted spoon – or, with swift strokes, baste the poori with the hot oil. In basting, what you actually do is push the hot oil towards and over the poori. Or you can do both of these things. But do it fast. Within half a minute, the poori should puff up. Turn it over with a slotted spoon, and cook another 30 seconds. Remove with slotted spoon, drain on paper towel, and serve immediately. If the first poori comes out hard, you are cooking it too long, or the oil is not hot enough, or both.

If you do not wish to serve the puffed-up pooris right away, deflate them as they come out of the *karhai* (watch out for that steam!) by pressing down on them; wrap tightly in a large sheet of aluminium foil. (Do not crush them, though.) As the pooris get done, lay them one over the other, and keep wrapping the lot with foil. This will keep them soft. If they are served this way, at room temperature, they are known as *baasi*, or 'stale', pooris. If you wish to reheat them, place the foil bundle in a 150°C (300°F) mark 2 preheated oven for 10 minutes.

To serve: Pooris go well with Kheema, with Lamb Cooked in Dark Almond Sauce, with Chicken Moghlai, and nearly all the vegetable dishes.

Paratha (whole-wheat griddle bread)

Makes 6 big parathas

---

115 g (4 oz) wheatmeal flour plus
   115 g (4 oz) plain flour or 225 g
   (8 oz) chapati flour

additional flour for dusting
1/2 tsp salt
about 9 tbsp vegetable oil

Put the flour and salt into a bowl. Dribble 2 tbsp of oil over the flour and rub it in with your fingertips. Slowly add about 175 ml (6 fl oz) plus 1 tbsp water, gathering the dough together into a ball as you do so. You should end up with a soft dough. Knead the dough for 10 minutes and then make a ball. Put the ball in a bowl and cover the bowl with a damp cloth. Set the dough aside for half an hour.

Knead the dough again and divide it into six parts. Keep five parts covered with a damp cloth as you work with the sixth. Make a round patty out of it and then roll it out on a floured surface until you have a 15 cm (6 inch) round. Dust with extra flour whenever necessary. Spread about 1 1/2 tsp oil on the top of this round. Gather the edges of the round together, forming pleats as you go. Soon you will have a closed pouch. Give the top of the pleats a small twist to close the pouch. Dust the pouch lightly with flour and put it, pleated side down, on a floured surface. Roll it out until it is about 18 cm (7 inches) in diameter. Heat a cast-iron griddle or frying pan over a medium-low flame. When hot, spread a tsp of oil on it and slap the *paratha* on to its heated surface. Cook for about 2 minutes. The top of the *paratha* should now have turned fairly pale. Spread a tsp of oil over it with the back of a spoon. Cook another minute or so, turning the heat down a bit if necessary. The first side should have developed some pale, reddish-brown spots. Turn the paratha over and cook the second side for about 3 to 3 1/2 minutes or until it, too, develops pale, reddish-brown spots. Take the paratha off the fire and wrap in aluminium foil. Make all the parathas this way, stacking them in the same aluminium-foil bundle. (Parathas may be reheated in the foil; place in a 180°C (350°F) mark 4 oven for about 15 minutes.)

Stuffed parathas (stuffed whole-wheat griddle breads)

Makes 8 parathas

225 g (8 oz) chapati flour or 115 g (4 oz) wheatmeal flour plus 115 g (4 oz) plain flour
additional flour for dusting
1/2 tsp salt plus some more for sprinkling
2 tbsp unsalted butter, cut into 6 pats
6 tbsp peeled, finely grated, and well-squeezed white radish

1/4 tsp garam masala
1/2 tsp ground cumin seeds
1/2–1 finely chopped fresh hot green chilli
1/4 tsp ground dried ginger
1 tbsp finely chopped fresh green coriander
1/4 tsp ajwain seeds
6 tbsp ghee or vegetable oil

Put the flour, 1/2 tsp salt and butter into the container of a food processor with the metal blade in place. Turn on the machine for 30 seconds. Now pour in 100 ml (4 fl oz) plus 3 tbsp water for the *chapati* flour and about 2 tbsp more for the wheatmeal mixture. Let the machine run until you have a ball of dough. Take the ball out and knead it for 10 minutes. You should have a soft but workable dough. If you do not have a processor, put the flour, salt and slightly softened butter into a bowl. Rub with your fingers until you have the consistency of fine bread crumbs. Add the same amount of water as above and gather into a ball. Knead for 10 minutes. Form a ball with the dough and put inside a bowl. Cover the bowl with a damp cloth and set aside for 1/2 to 1 hour.

Combine the white radish, garam masala, cumin seeds, green chilli, ginger and fresh coriander. Crush the *ajwain* seeds lightly in a mortar and add them to this mixture as well. This is the stuffing.

Heat a cast-iron griddle or a cast-iron frying-pan, about 20 cm (8 inches) in diameter over medium-low heat for about 10 minutes.

As the griddle heats, divide the dough into eight balls. Keep seven of them covered with cling film. Roll the eighth ball out on a floured board until it is 9 cm (3 1/2 inches) in diameter. Place a heaped teaspoon of stuffing in its centre. Sprinkle the stuffing with a little salt. Now gather the edges of the dough round and bring towards the centre, twisting them slightly to form a closed ball. Flatten the ball. Sprinkle it lightly with flour and roll out on a floured board until you have a 15 cm (6 inch) round.

Place the paratha on the heated griddle. Let it cook slowly until its underside develops light-brown spots. Turn and cook the same way on the other side. Now dribble 1 tsp of ghee along the edges of the paratha so it goes under it, and 1 tsp on top. Turn the paratha over again and cook for about a minute. Turn a fourth time and cook, slowly, another minute. In all, the paratha should cook about 5 minutes and not remain raw inside. It should also not burn, so adjust your heat accordingly. Wrap the paratha first in kitchen paper and then in a large piece of aluminium foil. Do all parathas this way, stacking them one on top of the other in the same piece of foil.

Bhatura

Serves 4

The *bhatura* is a bit like a deep-fried version of the naan. It is very popular in the Punjab as a 'snack' bread, eaten with spiced chickpeas.

---

140 g (5 oz) all-purpose white flour, plus a little extra flour for dusting
1/4 tsp baking powder
1 egg, beaten
1–1 1/2 tbsp plain yogurt

a little vegetable oil for brushing on dough
vegetable oil for deep frying, enough to have 6.5 cm (2 1/2 inches) in pot

---

Sift the 140 g (5 oz) flour and the baking powder into a bowl. Add the egg and begin to mix. Slowly add the yogurt and gather together the flour. Begin kneading. Add as much yogurt as will give you a soft dough. Knead dough for 10 minutes until it is smooth. Form into a ball, brush with oil, cover with damp cloth, and keep in a warm place for 3 hours.

With moistened hands, knead dough again.

Put oil in *karhai*, wok or other wide utensil for deep frying. Heat over medium flame. Allow oil time to get smoking hot.

Divide dough into 8 balls and cover with damp cloth. Take one ball at a time and flatten it. Flour the rolling surface. Roll out the ball into an 11.5 cm (4 1/2 inch) round, and drop it in when the oil is smoking. As it begins to sizzle, press down on it gently with the back of a slotted spoon. It will puff up. Turn it over and let other side brown lightly. The whole process should take about a minute. Do all bhaturas this way.

To serve: Serve hot with Chana Masaledar or any meat or vegetable dish.

Naan

Serves 6

Naan is a leavened flat bread shaped like a teardrop. It is best when cooked in the clay oven called the tandoor. While meats, chicken and fish grill on large skewers inside the tandoor, moistened naans are stuck to its walls to bake.

---

450 g (1 lb) all-purpose white flour
about 200 ml (7 fl oz) milk
1 egg, beaten
3/4 tsp salt
2 tsp sugar
1 tsp baking powder
1/2 packet dry yeast (11/2 tsp)

2 tbsp vegetable oil, plus a little
   more for brushing on dough later
4 tbsp plain yogurt
1/4 tsp black onion seeds (kalonji),
   or poppy seeds as substitute

Sift the flour into a bowl. Place the milk in a small pot and warm slightly. Remove from heat. In another bowl combine the egg, salt, sugar, baking powder, yeast, 2 tbsp oil, yogurt and 5 tbsp of the warm milk.

Mix well. Pour mixture over flour and rub it in with the hands.

Add 1 tbsp of warm milk at a time to the flour, and begin kneading. Add enough so that all the flour adheres and kneading is easy. You should have a soft dough. Knead well for about 10 minutes or until dough is elastic. Form into a ball, brush with oil, cover with damp cloth, and leave in a warm place to rise. If the temperature is above 27°C (80°F). it should take only 2 hours. Otherwise it may take about 3 hours.

Preheat grill.

Brush 3 baking trays lightly with oil.

Knead the dough again for a minute or two and divide into 6 balls. Flatten the balls one at a time, keeping the rest covered, and stretch them and pat them with your hands until you have a teardrop shape about 28 cm (11 inches) long and 10 cm (4 inches) wide. Do all balls this way, placing 2 naans on each baking tray as you do so. Cover with moistened cloths and leave for 15 minutes in a warm place.

Remove moistened cloths. Brush the centre portion of each naan with water, leaving a 1 cm (1/2 inch) margin. Sprinkle the centre portion with the onion or poppy seeds.

Place trays, one at a time, under the grill, about 6.5–7.5 cm (2½–3 inches) away from the heat and grill naans for about 2½ minutes on each side or until lightly browned.

To serve: Serve naans hot with Tandoori Chicken, Seekh Kabab, Lamb Cooked in Dark Almond Sauce, or Chicken Moghlai.

Rice-flour dosas with mustard seeds and black pepper

Makes 8 pancake-breads

The batter for these pancakes may be made almost entirely in a food processor or blender. It may also be made several hours in advance.

115 g (4 oz) plain white flour
140 g (5 oz) rice flour (also called rice powder)
⅛–¼ tsp cayenne pepper
115 g (4 oz) peeled and chopped onion
30 g (1 oz) freshly grated coconut
1¼ tsp salt

250 ml (8 fl oz) plain yogurt (the sourer the better)
about 7 tbsp vegetable oil
1 tsp whole black mustard seeds
¾–1 tsp coarsely crushed or very coarsely ground black peppercorns

Put the white flour, rice flour, cayenne, onion, coconut, salt, yogurt and 175 ml (6 fl oz) water into the container of a food processor or blender. Blend until smooth and pour into a bowl.

Heat 1 tbsp oil in a small frying pan or pot over a medium flame. When hot, put in the mustard seeds. As soon as the mustard seeds begin to pop (almost immediately), pour the seeds and oil over the batter. Add the black pepper and mix thoroughly.

See that you have everything you need for making the pancakes: an 18–20 cm (7–8 inch) nonstick frying-pan, a cup containing oil, a teaspoon, a rounded soup spoon for spreading out the batter, and a small measuring cup. You also need a plate to hold the pancakes and a second plate that you can invert over the first to keep the pancakes warm and moist.

Set the frying-pan over medium-low heat. Dribble ½ tsp oil into it. When the frying-pan is hot, pick up 75 ml (3 fl oz) of batter and plop it right in the centre of the frying pan. Immediately put the rounded bottom of a soup spoon very lightly on the blob of batter and, using a gentle but continuous spiral motion, spread the batter outwards. You should end up with a pancake 15–18 cm (6–7 inches) in diameter (the thinner, the better). Dribble 1/2 tsp of oil over the pancake and another tsp just outside its edges. Cover and cook for 31/2 to 5 minutes or until the pancake has turned a reddish-gold colour on the bottom and is slightly crisp along the edges. It may not colour uniformly. Remove the cover and turn the pancake over. Cook the second side uncovered until it, too, has developed reddish-gold spots, about 4 minutes. Remove with a spatula and keep on the nearby plate. Cover with the second inverted plate. Make all the pancakes this way, stacking them all on the same plate.

If you wish to reheat these pancakes cover them well in aluminium foil, and place in a 200°C (400°F) mark 6 oven for about 15 minutes.

Serve with Fresh Coconut Chutney or any vegetables of your choice.

Semolina idlis (savoury cakes)

Makes 12 small cakes

Idlis are a breakfast and snack food all over South India. They are round, slightly tart cakes, about 6.5–8 cm (21/2–3 inches) in diameter and about 2 cm (3/4 inches) thick in the centre.

Idlis need to be steamed over rapidly boiling water. The special steaming moulds used in South India are now available in Indian grocery stores. They consist of a central trunk on which several discs may be fitted at spaced intervals. Each disc is filled with tiny steam holes. It also has round depressions in it which act as moulds for the idlis. The entire 'tree' is placed over boiling water, covered and steamed.

If you cannot find the idli moulds, it is not hard to improvise. Use a steaming trivet, about 15 cm (6 inches) in diameter, and put it inside a colander. It will probably come to rest somewhere above the bottom of a rounded colander. Line the trivet and the sides of the colander with a double layer of wet cheesecloth. Pour a 1 cm (1/2 inch) thickness of batter into the cheesecloth, cover the colander, and then fold the over-hanging edges of cheesecloth over the lid so they do not burn. The colander should be set over a pot of boiling water in such a way that the water stays below the level of the idlis. Instead of ending up with lots of small idlis, you will have large cakes which you can cut up into diamonds, squares or wedges.

Whatever method of steaming you use, have plenty of extra boiling water at hand to replenish the water in your steamer.

---

2 tbsp vegetable oil plus a little
   more for greasing the moulds
1 tsp whole black mustard seeds
170 g (6 oz) semolina
3 tbsp freshly grated coconut

3/4 tsp salt
1–2 fresh hot green chillies, finely
   chopped
350 ml (12 fl oz) plain yogurt (the
   sourer the better)

Heat the 2 tbsp oil in a frying pan over a medium flame. When the oil is hot, put in the mustard seeds. As soon as the mustard seeds begin to pop, turn the heat to medium-low and put in the semolina. Sauté for 2 to 3 minutes. The semolina should not brown. Remove the frying-pan from the fire. Add the coconut, salt and green chillies. Mix and allow to cool somewhat. Add the yogurt and mix. You should have a thick batter.

Prepare your steaming apparatus and get the water to a rolling boil. (See note at the top of the recipe.) Oil the idli moulds and fill each with the batter. Cover and steam for 20 minutes. Ease each idli out with the help of a knife and serve hot with its smoother underside up.

CHUTNEYS, PICKLES AND OTHER RELISHES

No Indian meal is complete without at least one kind of relish. At its simplest, this can be a small, fresh, fiery green chilli, or it can be a hastily peeled and quartered onion. In lower-middle-class families, when the wife packs her husband's lunch in the early hours of the morning, she may not have any meat or vegetable to offer him with his *roti* (bread). What she will tuck in, though, with great love, ensconced between two *rotis*, will be a tiny portion of a sour spicy raw mango pickle! It may well be the climate that causes appetites to wilt and turn apathetic, especially during the blazing summer months. Relishes are, perhaps, just ways of prodding sluggish bodies into perking up and eating. At any rate, Indians seem to find them both desirable and necessary.

The recipes for most chutneys and pickles are usually handed down from mother to daughter, each family group specializing in its own particular varieties and styles. The result is that different families will serve you completely different sets of relishes. There are now a few companies that produce and bottle relishes, but at the moment they have not quite succeeded in tearing the Indian housewife away from her own home efforts. Some of these bottled relishes are available in delicatessens.

I have, very arbitrarily, I confess, divided relishes into three categories – chutneys, pickles and 'others'. 'Others' does not seem very dignified or very exotic, but you will begin to see my problem once I get to 'others'. Meanwhile, let me start with chutneys.

There are so many different kinds of chutneys – sweet chutneys, sour chutneys, sweet-and-sour chutneys, salty chutneys, hot chutneys, cold chutneys – the list could go on and on. The ingredients used in these chutneys can include tomatoes, ginger, onions, garlic, tamarind, bananas, mangoes, raisins, coconut, fresh coriander, fresh mint, lime juice, yogurt, vinegar, sugar, etc. Chutneys can be preserves – that is, they can be bottled and kept indefinitely like Sweet Tomato Chutney, or they can be made fresh daily, like Tamarind Chutney with Bananas or Fresh Mint Chutney with Fruit (see the following recipes). In our home we had a special woman who came in daily to grind the spices. When the spices were done, her second daily task was to grind the fresh green coriander chutney which we had at every meal.

Chutneys are generally served in small non-metallic bowls if they are to accompany a meal. Sometimes, however, they are used as a sauce to go over hot or cold foods. Food can also be cooked in a chutney or with a chutney. Some chutneys are eaten not as a relish but as a vegetable. In our family we eat a chutney made with the pulp of boiled green mangoes this way.

Pickles in India are a world in themselves. A whole book could be written about them. Pickles preserve, and in a land of warm climate and little refrigeration, almost everything gets pickled in order to prolong its life – hard berries, onions, raw mangoes, green chillies, cauliflower, carrots, turnips, limes, lemons, marrows, aubergines, mutton, prawns, lobsters, quail, partridge, bamboos, and what-have-you.

Pickling is generally done in oil, vinegar, water or lemon juice. Oil pickles can last for years, whereas water pickles have a limited life of 2 to 3 weeks, during which there are waxing, peak, and waning periods. Oil pickles can be hot and sour or hot and sweet (jaggery – or Indian molasses – often providing the sweetness). While ceramic or glass jars are used for oil pickles, the traditional water pickles are made in *mutkas*, round pots of half-baked clay. As the water pickle matures, it picks up an earthen flavour that is very refreshing. These pickles are sour (a bit like the gherkin and cucumber delicatessen pickles) and hot if you want them to be. Before each meal, a large bowl of the pickles, both water and vegetable, is removed from the earthenware pot and put to cool – in a refrigerator if there is one. This bowl is then brought to the table at mealtime. Each place setting has a cup or non-metallic bowl into which people serve themselves both the vegetable and the water.

Fresh ginger or green chillies can be pickled in lime juice. The juice is boiled first and then added to the ginger or the chillies.

Small boiling onions are often pickled in red vinegar. These are then lifted out of the vinegar and served with dishes like Tandoori Chicken.

There are, of course, many other relishes as well. And here we come to my category 'others'. Chopped or sliced onions, tomatoes and cucumbers are sprinkled with lime juice (or vinegar), salt, pepper and cayenne, and served in varying forms all over North India. Numerous dishes made with yogurt are also very popular. I feel Britain has still to discover the versatility of plain yogurt. At the moment, yogurt seems to provide nothing more than a quick lunch for the girl on a diet. Indians use yogurt as East Europeans use sour cream. Apart from cooking with it and using it as a marinade, we use it for hundreds of relishes. *Raitas* are one of them. Here cooked or raw vegetables are added to well-mixed yogurt, seasonings are sprinkled in, and the dish is cooled before being served.

Various 'dumplings' can also be made and put into yogurt. Since they never comprise a main dish, 'relish' is a very good word for them.

Sweet tomato chutney

Makes enough to fill 600 ml (1 pint) jar

I make this chutney with tinned tomatoes. You could, if you like, use fresh tomatoes when they are in season and really tasty. When cooked, this chutney is sweet and sour, thick and garlicky.

---

1 whole head of garlic, peeled and coarsely chopped

a piece of fresh ginger, about 5 cm (2 inches) long, 2.5 cm (1 inch) thick, and 2.5 cm (1 inch) wide, peeled and coarsely chopped

350 ml (12 fl oz) wine vinegar

2 x 400 g (14 oz) tins whole tomatoes (or 900 g (2 lb) fresh tomatoes prepared as suggested above)

340 g (12 oz) granulated sugar

1½ tsp salt

⅛–½ tsp cayenne pepper

2 tbsp golden raisins

2 tbsp blanched slivered almonds

Put the chopped garlic, ginger and 100 ml (4 fl oz) of the vinegar into the container of an electric blender and blend at high speed until smooth. In a 3.4 litre (6 pint) heavy-bottomed pot with non-metallic finish, place the tomatoes and juice from the tin, the rest of the vinegar, the sugar, salt and cayenne pepper (or, if you prefer, add the cayenne at the end, a little at a time, stirring and tasting as you do so). Bring to the boil. Add purée from the blender. Lower heat and simmer gently, uncovered, for about 1½ to 2 hours or until chutney becomes thick. (A film should cling to a spoon dipped in it.) Stir occasionally at first, and more frequently later as it thickens. You may need to lower the heat as the liquid diminishes. You should end up with about 600 ml (1 pint) of chutney, and it should be at least as thick as honey after it cools. If the tinned tomatoes you use have a lot of liquid in them, a longer cooking time may be required, resulting in a little less chutney.

Add the almonds and raisins. Simmer, stirring, for another 5 minutes. Turn heat off and allow to cool. Bottle. Keep refrigerated.

To serve: Since this is one of my favourite sweet chutneys, I always spoon out a small bowl of it for all my dinner parties. It goes with almost all foods and is *very* popular. Store, bottled, in the refrigerator. It keeps for months.

Fresh green chutney with coriander leaves and yogurt

Serves 6

This chutney needs to be made the day it is eaten. It can be served in a small bowl as a relish, or it can be served over meat, cooked fish, or vegetables. If pressed to classify it, I would call this a 'sour' chutney.

1 packed teacup chopped fresh
   green coriander
1 fresh hot green chilli, sliced, or
   1/4 tsp ground cayenne pepper
   (optional)
285 g (10 oz) plain yogurt

1 tbsp lemon juice
1/2 tsp salt (add more if you need it;
   the sourness of yogurt can vary
   with its age)
1/8 tsp freshly ground pepper
1/2 tsp roasted, ground cumin seeds

Put the green coriander and chilli in the container of an electric blender with 3 tbsp of water and blend until you have a smooth paste (you may need to push the coriander down a couple of times).

In a non-metallic bowl, combine the yogurt, salt, pepper, cumin, lemon juice and paste from the blender. Cover and refrigerate until ready to use.

To serve: Bring the cooled bowl to the table. You could serve it with almost any Indian meal. People should take just a tablespoon at a time.

Fresh mint chutney with fruit

Serves 6

1/3–1/2 well-packed teacup washed
   fresh mint leaves
4 tbsp lemon juice
2 fresh hot green chillies (use less
   or more as desired; as
   substitute, use 1/2 green pepper
   plus 1/2 tsp cayenne pepper)

1 medium-sized tart apple, peeled,
   cored and diced just before
   blending
1 orange, peeled, seeded and
   cubed
1 tsp salt

Combine all ingredients in the container of an electric blender. Blend at high speed until you have a smooth paste.

This chutney goes with most Indian foods. It is especially good with grilled Seekh Kabab, Tandoori Chicken, and Vegetable Pakoris.

Tamarind chutney with bananas

Serves 4–6

This is another sweet and sour chutney made with tamarind pulp. The addition of roasted cumin and slices of ripe bananas is, I think, very particular to Delhi dwellers.

Even though this chutney can be made a day in advance, it is best to add the banana slices just before serving. Banana slices that have spent a night in the refrigerator look very unhappy!

---

a piece of tamarind, the size of a tangerine
1–1½ tbsp sugar
1¼ tsp salt

1 tsp roasted, ground cumin seeds
⅛–¼ tsp cayenne pepper (optional)
1 ripe but firm banana

Since the tamarind generally comes in a large block, tear off a lump about the size of a tangerine. Soak it overnight in 175 ml (6 fl oz) hot water in a small non-metallic bowl or cup. (The water should cover the tamarind, so don't use a very wide bowl.) If you forget to do it overnight, do it first thing in the morning. All will not be lost! Soak it for a minimum of 4 hours.

Once it has soaked, mash down and break the lump in the water, making a thick, uneven pulp. I use my hands for this, but you could use the back of a wooden spoon.

Place a strainer over a non-metallic bowl, put the tamarind pulp in the strainer, and press down with the back of a spoon. Keep pressing until nothing but fibrous tissues and seeds are left in the strainer. Discard fibrous tissues and seeds. Make sure you scrape all the strained pulp on the outside of the strainer – it doesn't always drip down. Use extra water, if necessary, to separate all the pulp from the fibres.

Mix the strained pulp with the sugar, salt, cumin seeds and cayenne.

Slice a peeled banana into 0.5–1 cm (¼–⅓ inch) slices and mix with the tamarind pulp.

To serve: Put into small ceramic or glass serving bowl and place on the table along with other chutneys and pickles.

Fresh coconut chutney

Serves 6–8

1 teacup fairly well-packed, grated fresh coconut
½ teacup fairly well-packed, chopped fresh green coriander
1–2 fresh hot green chillies (use as desired)
a piece of fresh ginger, about 1 cm (½ inch) cube, peeled and chopped

1 clove garlic, peeled and chopped
6 tbsp plain yogurt
½ tsp salt
1 tsp lemon juice
1 tbsp vegetable oil
⅛ tsp urad dal (the hulled, split variety) grains
¼ tsp whole black mustard seeds

Put the coconut, green coriander, green chillies, ginger and garlic, along with 5 tbsp of water, into the container of an electric blender. Blend at high speed until you have a smooth paste, stopping occasionally to push down the ingredients.

Pour contents of blender into a bowl. Add yogurt, salt and lemon juice. Mix well.

In a 10–15 cm (4–6 inch) frying-pan, heat the oil. When very hot, put in the dal grains and mustard seeds. As soon as the dal darkens and the mustard seeds pop, pour contents of frying-pan into bowl with chutney. Mix well. Cover and chill until ready for use.

To serve: This South Indian chutney goes well with Vegetable Pakoris. It is also very good as a relish with most meals.

Apricot chutney with sultanas and currants

Makes about 900 ml (1½ pints)

In North India, we often make a chutney out of the flesh of a sour, dried plum known as *aloo bokhara* (the plum of Bokhara). I have changed that recipe somewhat and used dried apricots instead. I find that this sweet-and-sour, pectin-rich fruit makes a superb chutney.

450 g (1 lb) dried apricots	300 ml (1/2 pint) red wine vinegar
10 large cloves garlic, peeled and coarsely chopped	400 g (14 oz) sugar
	1/4 tsp salt
a 2.5 x 8 cm (1 x 3 inch) piece of fresh ginger, peeled and coarsely chopped	1/8–3/4 cayenne pepper
	85 g (3 oz) sultanas
	60 g (2 oz) currants

Put the apricots in a bowl. Pour 900 ml (1 1/2 pints) of hot water over them and let them soak for an hour.

Put the garlic and ginger into the container of an electric blender or a food processor along with 50 ml (2 fl oz) of the vinegar. Blend until smooth.

Empty the apricots and their soaking liquid into a heavy stainless steel or porcelain-lined pot. Add the garlic-ginger mixture, the remaining vinegar, sugar, salt and cayenne. Bring to the boil. Simmer on a medium flame, stirring frequently, for 45 minutes. Do not let the chutney catch at the bottom of the pot. Lower heat if necessary. Add the sultanas and currants and cook, stirring, for another half hour or until chutney takes on a thick, glazed look. (Remember that the chutney will thicken slightly as it cools.) Let the chutney cool and store, refrigerated, in lidded glass or ceramic jars.

Goan cabbage salad

Serves 4–6

The Goan peasants on the west coast of India eat this salad with many of their simple meals. Though carrots are not normally added to the salad, I find that they provide a nice contrast of colours. This salad gets sharper in taste as the days go on. It can be kept for several weeks.

340 g (12 oz) finely shredded cabbage	1-3 fresh hot green chillies, cut into fine, 4 cm (1 1/2 inch) long shreds
1 carrot, trimmed, peeled, and cut into 4 cm (1 1/2 inch) long julienne strips	600 ml (1 pint) distilled, white vinegar
	1 1/2 tbsp salt

Put the shredded cabbage, carrot and green chillies into a clean, wide-mouthed 1.1 litre (2 pint) jar. Mix the vinegar with the salt and pour that into the jar. Mix with a clean spoon. Cover, and leave for an hour.

Pickled green chillies

Makes enough to fill a 450 ml (³/₄ pint jar)

Here is my family's recipe for a fiery pickle that combines three of God's most potent creations – hot green chillies, cayenne and mustard. It is astoundingly good but only recommended for the stout of heart. There is no getting away from it – it is hot. It works wonders with all kinds of foods, perking up anything from cheese sandwiches to tomato salads.

---

225 g (8 oz) fresh hot green chillies
4 tbsp whole black mustard seeds
4 tbsp salt
1 tsp cayenne or other hot ground
    red pepper

a 2.5 cm (1 inch) cube of fresh
    ginger, peeled and finely
    chopped
2 tbsp mustard oil
3 tbsp lemon juice

Wipe each green chilli with a damp cloth. Spread out on a tray and leave to dry in a sunny or airy place.

Grind the mustard seeds to a powder in a coffee grinder or other spice grinder.

Trim away the stems of the green chillies and then slice them crosswise into 0.5 cm (¼ inch) thick rounds. (You may want to wear fine rubber gloves while doing this. If not, refrain from touching any part of your face before washing your hands thoroughly with soap and water.)

Combine the green chillies, ground mustard, salt, cayenne and ginger in a bowl. Mix well.

Heat the oil in a small frying pan or a very small pot over a medium flame. As soon as the oil begins to smoke, turn off the flame and let the oil cool completely. Pour the oil over the seasoned green chillies and mix well. Put the chilli mixture into a 450 ml (³/₄ pint) jar or crock and cover with a non-metallic lid. Put the jar in a warm sunny spot and let it get as many hours of sunlight as you can manage in the next 24 hours. Shake the jar a few times during this period.

On the following day, add the lemon juice. Put the lid back on and shake the jar thoroughly. For the next few days, put the jar out in a warm, sunny spot in the daytime and, if that spot is outdoors, bring the jar in at night. The pickle should take 3 to 4 days to mature in the summer and up to 7 days in the winter. The pickle is ready when it has turned slightly sour and the green chillies have lost their bright-green colour. It may now be refrigerated.

Carrots pickled in oil

Makes about 900 ml (1½ pints)
This is perhaps the simplest oil pickle you could make. It takes about a week to mature. It can then be refrigerated and kept for months.

2 tsp black mustard seeds	1 tsp cayenne pepper
450 g (1 lb) carrots of medium thickness	1 tsp ground turmeric
1 tsp salt	500 ml (16 fl oz) vegetable oil

Crush, pound or grind mustard seeds coarsely, so that they split at least in half, using either a heavy mortar and pestle or an Indian grinding stone, or a few quick spins of the electric coffee-grinder.

Peel the carrots. Cut off the coarse top and the bottom. Cut each carrot in 3 pieces. Halve or quarter these pieces lengthwise according to the thickness of the carrots.

Place carrots in clean, dry 900 ml (1½ pint) jar. Add salt, cayenne pepper, turmeric and crushed mustard seeds.

Warm the oil and pour over the carrots. Put lid on tightly and shake the jar well. Leave in a warm place for 7 days. Shake the jar once or twice daily.

To serve: Shake the jar. Remove one or two carrot pieces per person, and arrange in a small bowl or on relish tray. Do not serve the oil.

Onions pickled in vinegar

Makes about 900 ml (1½ pints)

This relish is served in Delhi's famous Moti Mahal restaurant. It is extremely simple to make. The onions need to marinate in the vinegar for at least 24 hours, so allow yourself sufficient time. In this recipe, I have made enough pickle to fill a 900 ml (1½ pint) jar. It should keep a month.

---

450 g (1 lb) white boiling onions (pick small, clean, even-sized onions)
500 ml (16 fl oz) red wine vinegar

2 cloves garlic, peeled and sliced
2 whole dried red peppers
1 tbsp salt

Peel onions. Slicing only three-quarters of the way down, quarter them lengthwise. Each onion should stay whole, with the four sections attached at the bottom. Place the onions in a clean, wide-mouthed 1.1 litre (2 pint) jar. You may have a few left over.

In a non-metallic bowl, combine the vinegar, garlic, red peppers and salt. Mix well. Pour this mixture over the onions to cover them. Put on a tight lid and set the jar aside for 24 hours.

The pickle is now ready. Refrigerate the jar. The onions can be taken out and eaten as and when desired.

To serve: Take as many of the onions out of the vinegar as you need and place them in a glass or other non-metallic bowl. They go well with Tandoori Chicken and Whole unhulled Urad and Rajma Dal.

Cucumber raita

Serves 4–6

This is a refreshing, cool yogurt and cucumber relish. In the hot summer months, it really takes the place of a salad.

---

1 cucumber
425 g (15 oz) plain yogurt
1 tsp salt
⅛ tsp freshly ground black pepper

½ tsp roasted, ground cumin seeds
⅛ tsp cayenne pepper (optional)
⅛ tsp paprika (for garnishing)

Peel and grate the cucumber.

Empty the yogurt into serving bowl and beat it well with a fork until it is smooth and paste-like.

Add the cucumber, salt, black pepper, roasted cumin (reserve a pinch for garnish) and cayenne to the bowl with the yogurt.

Sprinkle with paprika and the pinch of roasted cumin. Cover and refrigerate until ready to serve.

To serve: Bring bowl of cold yogurt to the table. This relish goes well with nearly all Indian meals.

Yogurt with roasted aubergine (baigan-ka-bharta)

Serves 4–6

---

1 medium-sized aubergine
425 g (15 oz) plain yogurt
1 small onion, peeled and finely minced
2 tbsp finely minced fresh mint
1 tsp salt

$1/8$–$1/4$ tsp freshly ground black pepper
$1/8$–$1/4$ tsp cayenne pepper (optional)
1 tsp freshly roasted, ground cumin seeds

Wash and wipe the aubergine. Line a burner with an aluminium protector if possible. Stand the aubergine directly on the gas burner and turn the flame on medium or medium low. Roast the aubergine on all sides, turning it over carefully. (For more detailed instructions, see Aubergine Bharta, page 91.) It should look fairly charred on the outside, and the inside should get soft and pulpy. This may take 20 to 25 minutes.

Peel the aubergine under cold running water, making sure all the blackened skin and the stem are removed. Now mince the pulp very finely and place in a bowl.

Empty yogurt into a serving bowl and mix well with fork. Add onion, mint, aubergine, salt, black pepper, cayenne and roasted cumin. Mix. Cover and refrigerate until ready to serve.

To serve: Serve cold as an hors d'oeuvre or as salad-type relish.

Cucumber and tomato with lemon juice

Serves 4

---

1 medium-sized cucumber
1 medium-sized tomato
1 tsp salt
1/8–1/4 tsp freshly ground black
    pepper

1 tsp roasted, ground cumin seeds
1–1 1/2 tbsp lemon juice
2 tbsp minced fresh green
    coriander
1/8 tsp cayenne pepper (optional)

Peel cucumber and dice it finely (about 0.5 cm (1/4 inch) cubes). Dice tomato as finely as cucumber. Combine all ingredients in serving bowl. Mix well. Cover and refrigerate for 30 minutes.

To serve: Bring cold serving bowl to table. This relish can be eaten with nearly all Indian meals.

Tomato and onion with lemon juice

Serves 4

---

1 medium-sized tomato
1 medium-sized onion
1 tsp salt
1/8–1/4 tsp freshly ground black
    pepper

1 tsp roasted, ground cumin seeds
1–1 1/2 tbsp lemon juice
1/8–1/4 tsp cayenne pepper

Dice tomato in 0.5 cm (1/4 inch) cubes. Peel and chop the onion. Combine all ingredients in serving bowl. Cover and refrigerate for 30 minutes.

To serve: Bring cold serving bowl to table. This relish can be eaten with nearly all Indian meals.

DESSERTS

In Europe and America, most meals end with dessert and coffee. In India most meals end with fruit – loquats, melons, watermelons, *cheekoos* and mangoes in the summer, and apples, oranges, bananas, guavas and pomegranates in the winter. These are often peeled at the table by the eldest woman of the house, and then passed around, always starting with the children. Desserts or 'sweets' are served mainly at very special luncheons and dinners, at snack time and tea time, and at religious festivals (which come extremely frequently!).

'Snack time' seems to have an unusually elevated place in Indian life. I remember when I was working in television shows in Delhi. We would be deep in rehearsal when, almost every hour, there would come a desperate cry from some corner of the studio: *'Quon bhai, chai hojai?'* ('Well now, brother, how about tea?'). Every actor and technician would stop (happily) in his tracks, and the whole group would saunter off to the nearest snack shop to have sweet and savoury snacks – and tea. The very spicy hot *samosas* and the sugar-sweet *gulab jamuns* were eaten simultaneously – a bit of one balancing a bite of the other and each swallowed with a soothing sip of scalding tea.

Tea has not always been drunk in India. Until the end of the last century it was more or less unknown in the subcontinent. With their sweet and sour snacks, Indians generally drank *shurbut* – fruit juice concentrates diluted with cold water – or hot, frothy milk. This milk was, and still is, sold by the snack vendor whose status often hinges upon how much froth he can raise. Since he has no frothing machine at his disposal, he achieves his bubbly result by briskly pouring the hot milk back and forth from one tumbler to another. These tumblers are first held close to each other. Slowly they are moved to a distance of several feet. The fast-flying milk never misses its mark and the stream of milk looks like white elastic being pulled between the tumblers. This sight is responsible for one of Delhi's oldest jokes, about the visitor from the old Northwest Frontier who asked if he might have 'two yards of that white thing' along with his other sweets!

Indian sweets tend to be *very* sweet. They tend also to be made of ingredients like vegetables (carrots, pumpkin), nuts (pistachios, almonds, coconut), flours (plain flour, rice flour, chickpea flour), and sweeteners (sugar, jaggery). But the most important ingredient is milk. Milk forms the base of more than half our sweets, and it is often milk in a form entirely unused in the West. Milk is boiled for hours until it forms a semi-solid dough called *khoya*. Most people do not make *khoya* at home. They go out and buy it. It is simpler. Since *khoya* is unavailable here, I have used several substitutes, powdered milk being one of them. For other desserts, milk is boiled down until it is half or a third of its original quantity.

Kulfi

Serves 6

This is Indian ice cream at its best. Milk is boiled down to a third of its original quantity. Sugar, cardamom and nuts are added, and the thickened milk is then poured into special conical containers and frozen. Traditionally, kulfi is served with *falooda*, a transparent vermicelli rather like the Japanese noodles in a sukiyaki.

1.4 litres (2½ pints) milk	3 tbsp sugar
4 whole cardamom pods	1 tbsp slivered unsalted pistachios

In a very heavy-bottomed pot, boil milk down to 500 ml (16 fl oz) stirring it every few minutes. This may take up to 1½ hours. After the first hour, lightly crush 2 of the cardamom pods and add them to the milk.

When the milk has boiled down to 500 ml (16 fl oz) turn off heat. Remove and discard cardamom pods. Add sugar and nuts. Stir well.

Grind the seeds from the other 2 cardamom pods and add them to the milk. Leave milk to cool.

When cool, stir once and pour milk equally into six 75 ml (3 fl oz) or 100 ml (4 fl oz) paper cups, or similar containers, or a bowl. Cover with aluminium foil and freeze. Stir the kulfi every 20 to 30 minutes to help break up the crystals. It will get harder to stir as it thickens. When it becomes too thick to stir, leave to freeze solid. Keep covered.

To serve: Run a warm knife along the inside of each cup or container to remove the kulfi. (You may need to pour warm water on the outside to loosen it.) Serve individual portions on small chilled plates.

Gajar-ka-halva

Serves 8

In this carrot halva, the carrots are completely unrecognisable. Milk and grated carrots are cooked until they become a dryish homogeneous mass. Sugar (and, if you like, lightly fried raisins and nuts) are then added, and the dish is served warm or at room temperature.

---

900 ml (1½ pints) milk
900 g (2 lb) carrots, peeled and grated
2 cardamom pods
10 tbsp vegetable oil
3 tbsp sugar

1 tbsp each lightly fried raisins and almonds (optional)
300 ml (½ pint) clotted or double cream (optional)

Put the milk, grated carrots and cardamom pods in a 25 cm (10 inch) heavy-bottomed pot. Bring to the boil. Lower heat to medium and cook, stirring occasionally, until no liquid is left. This may take about 30 minutes.

Add the oil, turn the heat down slightly, and start frying the carrot-milk mixture, stirring *all the time*. Continue until the carrots turn a reddish-brown. This may take 30 to 40 minutes.

Add sugar and, if you like, raisins and almonds. Cook, stirring, another 2 minutes. Turn off heat. Allow halva to cool. Cover and refrigerate until ready to eat.

To serve: This halva can be warmed or served at room temperature. In India, it is often served with clotted cream – the cream that forms when unhomogenized milk is boiled. You could, if you like, serve it with heavy cream just lightly whipped so it doubles in bulk.

Whole-wheat halva

Serves 6

This simple, quick-cooking halva contains one of the most nourishing food combinations – whole grains (whole-wheat flour), nuts (pistachios, cashews and almonds), dried fruit (sultanas), and dairy products (butter and milk). It is also an excellent snack or dessert for growing children and active adults.

---

115 g (4 oz) unsalted butter
1 tbsp blanched, slivered almonds
1 tbsp pistachios, slivered
1 tbsp coarsely chopped raw
cashews

1 tbsp sultanas
125 g (4½ oz) whole-wheat flour
6½ tbsp sugar, or to taste
750 ml (1¼ pints) scalding hot milk

Take a square cake-tin, about 20 x 20 x 4 cm (8 x 8 x 1½ inches), and grease the inside lightly with butter. Set the tin aside.

Put the remaining butter into a 20–25 cm (8–10 inch), heavy-bottomed frying-pan and melt on medium-low heat. As soon as the butter melts, put in the almonds, pistachios, cashews and sultanas. Stir until the nuts turn a shade darker and the sultanas swell. Do not let the butter burn. Add the whole-wheat flour and stir gently for about three minutes or until the flour is no longer raw and is lightly roasted. It will give off a wonderful smell of roasted wheat. Add the sugar and mix well. Add the scalding hot milk. Stir and mix. Cook, stirring, for another minute or so.

Empty the contents of the frying-pan into the buttered cake tin. Spread the halva and pat down evenly. Allow to cool. Cover with cling film until ready to eat.

Remove cling film and cut halva into 4 cm (1½ inch) cubes or diamond shapes. Serve at room temperature. This halva may also be served warm, shortly after it is made.

Grilled bananas

Serves 4

1 tbsp melted butter	3 tbsp orange juice
2 very firm large bananas	2 tbsp brown sugar
1 tsp lemon juice	1 tbsp blanched slivered almonds

Preheat the grill.

Brush a small, flameproof baking dish (a small baking tray will do) with half the butter. Split the bananas in half, lengthwise, and lay them in the dish. Mix the lemon and orange juice and pour it over the bananas. Brush the bananas with the remaining butter, and sprinkle with brown sugar.

Place under grill for about 4 minutes or until bananas are lightly browned. Sprinkle almond slivers over bananas and put them under the grill for another minute or two, or until almonds are browned. Remove from grill.

To serve: Serve the bananas hot. This dish should be prepared just before eating.

Fried dates

Serves 4–6

This simple dessert is popular among the Bohris of Gujarat. If you like dates and chewy, sticky caramely things, you will love this. It takes just a few minutes to make and should be cooked just before serving.

3 tbsp vegetable oil	1 tbsp slivered unsalted pistachios
225 g (8 oz) pitted good-quality dates	300 ml (1/2 pint) clotted or double cream

Heat the oil in a 25 cm (10 inch) frying-pan over a medium flame. When hot, put in the dates. Stir them around for 10 to 20 seconds. Remove with slotted spoon and place in serving dish.

Add pistachios to cream and put in serving pitcher.

To serve: Pass around the dates as well as the pitcher with the cream and nuts. The cream should be poured over the hot dates.

Malpua

Serves 6

This is a pancake immersed in a sugar syrup.

---

170 g (6 oz) sifted all-purpose white
    flour
100 ml (4 fl oz) milk
175 ml (6 fl oz) double cream

600 g (1¼ lb) sugar
2 cardamom pods, slightly crushed
3 tbsp vegetable oil (more may be
    needed)

Mix the flour, milk and cream with a whisk. Cover and refrigerate overnight.

Make the syrup by combining the sugar, 500 ml (16 fl oz) of water, and the cardamom pods in a pot. Bring to the boil without stirring. Lower heat and simmer 2 to 3 minutes, or until all the sugar dissolves. Put syrup into serving bowl large enough to hold pancakes as well.

Heat the oil in a 25–30 cm (10–12 inch) frying-pan over a medium flame. Pour in enough batter to make two 10–12 cm (4–5 inch) pancakes at a time. Cook pancakes slowly on both sides so they get golden-brown and crisp. As pancakes are done, lift them out and put them into the syrup. Finish all the batter this way. Adjust heat so as not to burn pancakes, and add more oil as you require it. There should be about 3 tbsp of oil in the frying-pan constantly.

Malpua can be served either at room temperature or slightly warm. Bring bowl of pancakes and syrup to table and let your guests serve themselves.

Kheer

Serves 4

This is my mother's recipe for *kheer*, a dessert made with milk and rice.

When my mother made the kheer she set it in shallow half-baked earthenware bowls called *shakoras*. As a result, it picked up the delicious fragrance of freshly moistened earth. You could serve your kheer in individual custard bowls or, if you prefer, you could put it all in one shallow bowl from which each person would serve himself.

1.1 litres (2 pints) milk
1 tbsp long-grain rice
4 whole cardamom pods, slightly
   crushed
2 tbsp sugar

10 pistachios, unsalted and
   slivered, plus a few more for
   garnishing
vark (fine sheets of red, silver or
   gold foil), if available

Combine the milk, rice and cardamom pods in a heavy-bottomed pot. Bring to the boil. Lower heat and reduce milk until you have 600 ml. (1 pint) This may take about 1¼ hours. Turn off heat.

Remove cardamom pods and discard. Add sugar and nuts. Mix well. Leave to cool.

Mix again. Pour into serving bowl. Decorate with vark, if using. Sprinkle a few more slivered pistachios on top of the vark. Cover and refrigerate until ready to serve.

Gulab jamun

Serves 6–8

This is a simple, very sweet dessert which can be served warm or at room temperature. It is made with dried milk. You could call it 'fried milk balls in syrup'.

900 g (2 lb) granulated sugar
3 cardamom pods, slightly crushed
170 g (6 oz) powdered milk
85 g (3 oz) all-purpose white flour
100 ml (4 fl oz) vegetable oil or
   melted ghee

100 ml (4 fl oz) milk
vegetable oil for deep frying,
   enough to have 7.5 cm (3 inches)
   in cooking pot

First make the syrup. In a 3.4 litre (6 pint) pot, combine 1 litre (1¾ pints) water, the sugar and the cardamom. Lower heat. Simmer 2 to 3 minutes, or until all the sugar has been dissolved. Do not stir.

Pour half the syrup into a serving bowl (about a 2.3 litre (4 pint) size). Leave the other half in the pot, with the cardamom pods.

Combine the powdered milk, flour, oil and milk in a bowl. Make a soft dough. Make small, smooth balls out of the dough, each about 2.5 cm (1 inch) in diameter. You should be able to make more than 2 dozen jamuns.

Heat oil for deep frying in wok, karhai or any heavy-bottomed wide pot. You should have at least 7.5 cm (3 inches) of oil. Keep on *low* flame. The jamuns need to be fried slowly.

Put a jamun into the oil as a test. If it begins to brown immediately, your heat is too high. Each jamun should take 4 to 5 minutes to get a reddish-brown colour on all sides. If the first jamun does not turn out right, correct the heat. It is better to take this precaution than have a whole batch burn outside and stay raw inside.

Now put in 6 jamuns at a time. Turn them over as they turn reddish-brown on one side. As they get fried, put them into the syrup in the pot. Bring this syrup to the boil. Let each batch simmer in the syrup for 5 minutes. When the jamuns are 'syruped', lift them out with a slotted spoon and place them in the fresh syrup in the serving bowl. Keep frying and 'syruping' a batch at a time – as one batch fries, another can 'syrup' – until they are all done. When cool, cover serving bowl and refrigerate. The syrup in the pot can now be discarded.

To serve: Gulab jamuns can be served cold, at room temperature, or slightly warmed. Remember, you serve yourself only the gulab jamun, not the syrup in the bowl!

Besan barfee (gram-flour fudge)

Makes 144 little cubes

---

180 g (6 oz) gram flour
250 ml (8 fl oz) vegetable oil
400 g (14 oz) sugar
1/2 tsp ground cardamom seeds

2-3 tbsp unsalted pistachios, lightly
    crushed
1–2 tbsp coarsely chopped
    blanched almonds

Sift the gram flour. Heat the oil in a heavy, 25–30 cm (10–12 inch) frying-pan, wok or sauté pan over a medium flame. Put in the sifted gram flour. Stir and fry for 2 to 3 minutes or until flour turns a shade darker and is cooked (it should taste fried, not raw). Put the flour into a large bowl, stir once, and allow to cool.

Make a syrup with 250 g (8 fl oz) water and the 400 g (14 oz) sugar by bringing the water-sugar combination to the boil and then simmering very gently for about 20 minutes or until the syrup reaches a one-thread consistency. (To test this, dip in a wooden spoon and let coat slightly. Pinch some syrup off the back of the spoon with two fingers and then try separating the fingers. One sticky thread should form. This is the Indian method. If you have a better one, use it.)

Pour the hot syrup into the cooled gram-flour mixture. Add the ground cardamom seeds and the nuts, and mix well. Keep stirring until mixture begins to harden slightly. (It should still be pourable.) Pour into a 23 cm (9 inch) square cake tin, tilt tin so barfee mixture flows to the edges, and allow to cool. Cut into 2 cm (3/4 inch) cubes.

Besan Barfee, if tightly wrapped in aluminium foil and then placed in plastic containers, freezes very well.

INDEX